Contents

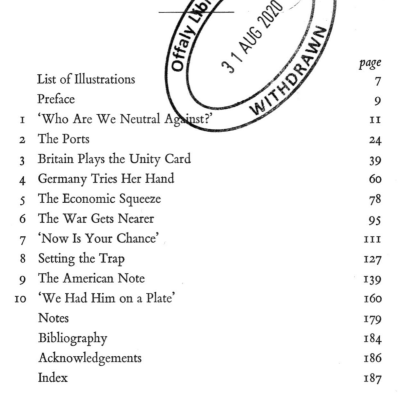

List of Illustrations

———◆———

IN TEXT

Preface

———————◆———————

It was and still is a hoary joke in Ireland to ask 'Where were you in 1916?' (the year of the Easter Rebellion) and to receive the cynical reply 'Under the bed.' But no one ever asks 'Where were you in 1939?' Why should they? Ireland was neutral thanks to God and de Valera, and what more was there to be said? Belatedly I became curious about our neutrality: how it was decided, how it was maintained and how did it conform to the lofty moral image we have of ourselves in international relations – spearheading the break-up of the British Empire, helping to democratise the Commonwealth, pleading for the collective security ideal in the League of Nations, modestly aiding war refugees, advocating in the United Nations the renunciation of nuclear arms, peacekeeping in the Congo and Cyprus and so on.

It is difficult to find out much about Irish neutrality in World War II. The newspapers of the time were severely censored, the Dail was told practically nothing by the government of the day of how neutrality was being implemented, de Valera's numerous speeches are remarkably uninformative, most senior officers of the defence forces who are still alive regard themselves as bound by the Official Secrets Act, politicians who survive often go blank when prompted to stir their memories about the period while being ready to give vivid accounts of events during the War of Independence which was twenty years earlier. No government papers for the period are available and there are doubts as to whether they even exist.

At last (in 1972) the British government opened the war cabinet and related papers for the whole war period. It seemed a rare opportunity to turn up some at least of the elusive record of Irish neutrality about which there has been such an official reticence. The story that follows is, therefore, not complete but if it helps to shed further light on a dim chapter in modern Irish history it will have been worthwhile.

Chapter 1

'Who Are We Neutral Against?'

A thunderstorm burst over Dublin early on the morning of Sunday, 3 September 1939, the day Britain and France declared war on Germany. The Dail and the Seanad, the two houses of parliament, had sat until after 5 am to declare a 'national emergency' and rush through the Emergency Powers Bill giving the government dictatorial powers to secure the public safety and preservation of the state. The deputies and senators emerging from Leinster House to go to 6 am Mass before going home for their breakfast, had to make their way through flooded streets.

On that same wet and dismal Sunday several British Royal Air Force seaplanes on patrol in the Irish Sea got into difficulties because of the weather; two landed at the holiday resort of Skerries ten miles north of Dublin and another off Dun Laoghaire, south of Dublin. Technically it was a breach of Irish neutrality, but at this early stage in the war nobody was quite sure what to do about it. The Department of Defence toyed with the idea of internment to the horror of some senior officers at Army headquarters who foresaw an angry British reaction. The dilemma was solved by a clearance in the weather which helped the planes to make their getaway. Naturally, the incident had attracted a lot of local interest and is believed to have prompted the immortal remark, 'Who are we neutral against?' which was picked up in the international press and seemed at that time to reflect the widespread doubts about how neutrality was going to work in practice. Ireland, after all, depended almost exclusively on Britain for her overseas trade and the six north-eastern counties, as an integral part of the United Kingdom known as Northern Ireland, were at war with Germany. The Anglo-Irish Treaty of 1921 which partitioned the country gave the other twenty-six counties, to be known as the Irish Free State, Dominion status.

That night Mr de Valera broadcast to the nation. He announced a small cabinet reshuffle and went on to say:

> Noting the march of events your Government decided its policy early last Spring and announced its decision to you and the world. We resolved that the aim of our policy would be to keep our people out of a war. I said in the Dail that with our history, with our experience of the last war, and with part of our country still unjustly severed from us, we felt that no other decision and no other policy was possible.

But Irish neutrality did not appear quite so cut and dried in London where the previous Friday, the day Germany invaded Poland, the cabinet was told by Mr Chamberlain that he had received a communication from Mr de Valera about the latter's meeting with the German Minister in Dublin, Dr Edouard Hempel. If war broke out, Hempel told de Valera, Germany was anxious to respect the neutrality of Eire. The Secretary of State for the Dominions, Sir Thomas Inskip (later to become Lord Caldecote), then said that it had been contemplated that at the least Britain should ask Eire to break off diplomatic relations with Germany if Britain became involved in war. The Irish High Commissioner in London, Mr John Dulanty, had informed Inskip that he thought that 'in a week Eire would come in on our side as a result of attacks on shipping'.[1]

It is curious, if Inskip's report is accurate, that Dulanty should have expressed such a pessimistic view of Ireland's chances of remaining neutral while in Dublin all resources were being mobilised to maintain neutrality as long as was humanly possible. But in fact Dulanty was only reflecting the doubts expressed by de Valera himself seven months earlier during the Dail debate on the defence estimate.[2]

On the instructions of Ribbentrop, his foreign minister, Hempel called on de Valera on 31 August, the eve of the outbreak of war. It is not surprising that de Valera, having expressed Ireland's desire for peace with all nations including Germany, then went on to point out the evident difficulties arising out of the narrowness of the Irish Sea and the vital importance to Ireland of maintaining her trade with

Britain. The Irish government would have to show a certain consideration for Britain which, in similar circumstances, they would also show
for Germany. He was explicit in his discussions of the dangers to Irish
neutrality. These he saw as possible violations of territorial waters by
either side, action against the partitioned area and the exploitation by
Germany of the 'anti-British radical nationalist group' (euphemism for
the IRA). He warned Hempel of the possible consequences of German
action along any of these lines.[3]

This little phrase 'a certain consideration for Britain' turned out to
be the key to Irish neutrality, and Hempel could scarcely have guessed
at the extent to which ostensible neutrality would be bent in favour of
Britain as the war progressed. Even before the war had broken out,
discussions had taken place between the two countries on possible
measures of co-operation such as censorship, a coast-watching service,
control of broadcasting and navigation lights.[4] The use of the German
legation in Dublin as a channel for espionage reports to Berlin was one
of the preoccupations of the British security forces in the early months
of the war, and they moved swiftly to plug the gap with the full co-
operation of the Irish authorities. By November the war cabinet had
been told that Eire had agreed to the re-routing of the two cables to
the USA through London, and the German minister had been told not
to send cipher messages. (This was denied to the author in 1973 by a
member of the legation during the war.) A third cable linking Ireland
with Le Havre was also effectively under the control of the British
chief censor and a telephone censorship between Britain and Ireland,
north and south, was set up at Liverpool.[5]

Despite these favours conceded by de Valera, which he could justify
as putting into practice his frequent pledge that he would never allow
Ireland to be used as 'a base for attacking Britain', the belligerent who
was at the greatest disadvantage in Dublin at the outbreak of the war
was in fact Britain as she had no mission or diplomatic representative
in Ireland, and the British Trade Commission in Merrion Square was
hardly an adequate substitute at such a critical time.

To all intents and purposes, Mr de Valera's constitution of 1937
turned Ireland from a dominion into a republic, but without the word
being mentioned once. There was an important reason for this ambiguity. The Constitution Amendment Bill, passed at the time of the
King Edward VIII abdication crisis, had removed all reference to the

king from the Free State Constitution, and the External Relations Act allotted the crown the strictly limited role in external affairs of signing letters of credence of diplomatic and consular representatives and of concluding international agreements on the advice of the government. This tenuous link of 'external association' with the British Commonwealth was retained so as to facilitate the reunification of Ireland at some future date, and so the 1937 constitution was careful not to break the link.

The new name for the new state was to be 'Ireland' in English and 'Eire' in Gaelic, but the territory designated by these names was the whole island and a formal claim to the partitioned six counties was thus made. But realism was shown in the provision that 'pending the re-integration of the national territory', the jurisdiction of the new state would cover the twenty-six counties only. This was all right in theory, but in practice there was bound to be confusion over the use of these names. The British government rejected the claim to the six counties and began to use 'Eire' as a term in English for the twenty-six counties. This practice was widely adopted even by Irish newspapers but not, of course, by Mr de Valera's *Irish Press*. The British government, although taken aback by the undoubtedly republican nature of the new constitution, declared somewhat optimistically that it did not effect 'a fundamental alteration' in Irish membership of the British Commonwealth. But the divergence of Irish and British views was to be shown over the disagreement about what to call the official British representative in Dublin. London thought he should be addressed as High Commissioner, as was the case for the other Dominions, but Mr de Valera said he should be a minister thereby affirming the country's independence from imperial trappings.

Having declared Irish neutrality, de Valera's major preoccupation was to neutralise the IRA who would naturally see in England's difficulty Ireland's opportunity. In fact, since the previous January the IRA had been officially at war with Britain following the delivery of an ultimatum by the self-styled 'Government of the Irish Republic' demanding the removal of British forces from Northern Ireland within four days. The ignoring of the ultimatum led to the outbreak of the IRA bombing campaign in Britain in tube stations, cinemas, hotels, pillar-boxes and even in Madame Tussaud's Chamber of Horrors. The toll of lives was mercifully light until the explosion in Coventry on 25

August in a crowded shopping street in which five persons were killed and over sixty injured. One of the IRA bombers sent over to Britain after the start of the war was Brendan Behan, then only sixteen, and his arrest and imprisonment were later memorably recorded in *Borstal Boy*.

The German military secret service, the Abwehr, was already setting up a courier and communications system with the IRA, while a sabotage campaign was being planned for Northern Ireland.[6] The Fianna Fail government had already moved against the IRA, many of whom were former republican comrades from the civil war period, and it had been proscribed as an 'illegal organisation' following the passing of the Offences Against the State Act in June 1939. The IRA, with their virulent anti-British philosophy, were a serious threat to Irish neutrality at the outbreak of war, and de Valera knew he would be watched closely by these extremists for any sign of favour towards Britain which they could exploit as a sell-out of the Catholic nationalists in the north.

The war was only a few days old, therefore, when de Valera sent the Secretary of the Department of External Affairs, Mr Joseph Walshe, to London with a message for the new Secretary of State for the Dominions, Mr Anthony Eden. Mr de Valera had retained the external affairs portfolio for himself as well as being head of the government since coming to power in 1932, and as Ireland's representative at the League of Nations Assembly meetings he had come to know Eden fairly well.

Walshe went to see Eden accompanied by the Irish High Commissioner in London, Mr John Dulanty, who curiously enough had worked for Churchill in his election campaign in Manchester in 1906 and as a senior civil servant in Churchill's Ministry of Munitions in World War I. Walshe told Eden, according to the latter's report, that de Valera felt that some emphatic statement of Eire's neutrality was essential from the point of view of political conditions in Eire and that while the government and the great majority of the people of Eire were anxious to do what they could to help Britain and would in fact do so, it was essential in Eire's interests that the small but active and irresponsible minority who were implacably hostile to Britain should be given no loophole for creating difficulties.[7]

This meeting did not prepare Eden for the shock of the *aide-mémoire* which Dulanty handed him on 12 September in which the Irish government announced the prohibition against vessels of war and submarines of the belligerent powers using Irish territorial waters and ports, and also forbade the use of Irish airspace to military aircraft belonging to the belligerents. The prohibitions were based on international law and were to be given effect by appropriate government orders. In a memorandum to the war cabinet, Eden said he had been advised that the restrictions were not 'an unreasonable exercise of authority' but he felt it would be wrong to acquiesce in them without making an effort to try and make them 'less embarrassing from our point of view'. As it happened, Sir John Maffey, who had been asked to come out of retirement to fill the post of United Kingdom Representative in Eire if Mr de Valera would agree, was about to make a preliminary visit to Dublin and Eden asked him if he could obtain a further insight into de Valera's attitude on this question.

Maffey had enjoyed only five years of retirement after an outstanding career in the colonial service when he was asked to take on the delicate mission in Dublin. He had been educated at Oxford and the German university of Marburg, where he had studied phonetics. He joined the Indian civil service in 1900 and nine years later was appointed political agent at the Khyber. In 1916 he became private secretary to the Viceroy, Lord Chelmsford, and later Chief Commissioner of Peshawar where he distinguished himself by his negotiations with the Afridis tribe to secure the release of a Miss Mollie Ellis who had fallen into their hands. In 1925 Maffey was appointed Governor-General of the Anglo-Egyptian Sudan and served there until retirement in 1934. It was during this time that Maffey made a report on the situation in Abyssinia which appeared sympathetic to Italian claims in the area. Not long after Maffey's appointment, Hempel referred to this report in one of his despatches to Berlin with the implication that Maffey might be able to play a role in the peace overtures which were being made with Italian support following the crushing of Poland.

The only recorded peace feelers came a few months later from the rather eccentric Lord Tavistock, a former communist but later strongly attracted by fascism and the nazis. He embarrassed Hempel in March 1940 when he published a leaflet setting out alleged German peace terms which, he said, he had obtained from the German legation in Dublin through 'an Irish friend'. The legation immediately denied handing over any peace conditions to Tavistock who had come to Dublin with the knowledge of the British government the previous January. Hempel had refused to see him but allowed the counsellor, Thomsen, to talk to him and he had limited himself to references to the 'German point of view as laid down in the well-known German official declaration.' Tavistock later became Duke of Bedford.

Maffey stood an impressive 6ft 4in, and Kees Van Hoek of the *Irish Independent*, who interviewed him, described him as 'a miracle of youthful virility' with a clear and rapid deep voice, a full crop of long grey hair, a long strong nose, tight-lipped mouth and sparkling eyes under straight full eyebrows. His daughter, Penelope, who accompanied him to Dublin was married to Lord Beaverbrook's nephew who was a pilot in the RAF. Neither Maffey's long colonial service nor family ties would have disposed him to a favourable view of Irish independence or neutrality, but as a superb diplomat he knew how to keep his feelings well under control.

Maffey's first meeting with de Valera was on 14 September in Government Buildings in Merrion Street. At Irish insistence he had travelled to Dublin under the pseudonym of Harrison and was told to ask for the Department of Agriculture. The Department of External Affairs had not at that period moved to its present quarters of Iveagh House on St Stephen's Green and was housed on a floor of the Department of Agriculture. Nevertheless the pseudonym and misleading address were clumsy subterfuges which showed the extent of Irish nervousness where contacts with Britain were concerned and respect, perhaps, for the IRA's intelligence network.[8]

The meeting lasted two and a half hours, and the two men were alone except for a few minutes at the end when Walshe came in. Maffey has left a splendid account which merits being given at some length as an indication of how de Valera's mind was working at that time.[9]

Mr de Valera spoke with emphasis of the difficulties in the way of appointing a 'United Kingdom Representative', that is to say of creating an appointment of a new and special character. The shout would be raised of 'Dublin Castle back again' and it would be a battle cry for the IRA and extremists. It was true he had considered the idea but when he came closer to it and saw more of the forces working against him he had sensed a danger. He spoke at some length of the

B

difficulties of his position, his every action studied by men bitterly opposed to any sort of rapprochement with the United Kingdom, critical of any wavering from the straight path of neutrality. 'All this happens because you maintain the principle of partition in this island!' He pointed to a map of Ireland hanging on the wall before him: 'Eire Jet-black, Northern Ireland a leprous white.'

Maffey begged that the Irish *aide-mémoire* should not be published. These restrictive rules in that crude form would excite much feeling in England, particularly in view of their action in surrendering the Irish ports so recently. It would be adding to Mr Chamberlain's difficulties. This argument evidently touched the president at once. He expressed the deepest admiration for and sympathy with the prime minister. He said 'He has done everything that a man could do to prevent this tragedy.' (Maffey's plea on this matter was successful as the Emergency Powers Order on belligerent ships and aircraft was not published until over a year later when Churchill made a bellicose speech about the ports.)

On the subject of neutrality of Eire, Mr de Valera said that two-thirds of his people were pro-British, or at any rate anti-German, at that time. But there was a very active minority. Personally he had great sympathy with England. But though the cause of Poland was their *casus belli* the reasons for the breach went deeper than that and motives which affected England could not affect Eire. Maffey replied that in this struggle at last there was an ideal for which England and Eire could stand together and from that association a new chapter in their history could start. But this brought de Valera back on the partition of Ireland. Why did not the prime minister put his foot down and stop the follies and oppressions of Northern Ireland? Look at what a picture they might have! A united, independent Ireland! Think of the effect in America where the Irish element had ruined and would ruin any possibility of Anglo-American understanding! Why could they not see where the flaw in their armour lay? It was not a matter of religion. The Protestant minority in Eire were happy and contented. The Northern Ireland element would be of real use to England as a part of the whole body politic of the island. The petty tyrannies and oppressions going on in Northern Ireland must lead to disaster. 'If I lived there,' he exclaimed with heat, 'I should say "I'll be damned if I'll be ruled by these people".'

Back in London, Eden was struggling with the dilemma posed by Irish neutrality and he analysed the problem at some length for the war cabinet in a memorandum on 16 September:[10]

On the constitutional side the question of any formal recognition by this country of the neutrality of Eire presents a serious difficulty. We do not want formally to recognise Eire as a neutral while Eire remains a member of the British Commonwealth. To do this would be to surrender the hitherto accepted constitutional theory of the indivisibility of the Crown. Equally we do not want to take the line that Eire is no longer a member of the British Commonwealth. This would involve the rejection of the policy followed with the assent of the other Dominions since the establishment of the new Constitution of Eire in 1937 and would moreover have serious repercussions in many directions, e.g. the status under United Kingdom law of individual Irishmen.

Eden said there were three courses of action possible. The first was to refuse to accept the Eire memorandum on shipping restrictions and reserve the right to take the necessary measures to suppress enemy submarine activity whether within Eire territorial waters or not. But the objections to this course were that it might provoke an open breach with Eire 'which again might have unfortunate reactions on neutral and particularly United States opinion'. The second course was to accept in substance and tacitly the Eire rules but to suggest that it would be sufficient to frame them in more general terms. The third course would be to accept such modified rules on condition that in cases of infringement by enemy vessels of the rules, Britain reserved the right to supplement any action which the Eire government would take to deal with such vessels and prevent them from using Eire ports and territorial waters as a base for an attack on Britain. In this connection, Eden also had the clever idea of making use of a statement by de Valera himself in the Dail on 19 May 1937 that 'it would be our duty to do everything in our power to see that no foreign country got a foothold on our soil ... it is quite obvious that the people in Britain ... would have to give us the assistance which we, for our own sakes, would be anxious to call for, provided it was clear that the whole object of it was to maintain the inviolability of our territory'. Eden concluded by saying he favoured the third course and if the war cabinet approved he proposed asking Maffey to return to Dublin with letters from the prime minister and himself and to try and reach an agreement with Mr de Valera on

the lines indicated. Thus Maffey should press strongly for the establishment of a resident representative in Dublin who would co-ordinate
matters and pass on to the Admiralty the information obtained from
the Eire coast-watching service. But there must continue to be firm
resistance to diplomatic nomenclature for such a post.

The war cabinet duly agreed on 18 September, with Churchill
growling that the position was 'profoundly unsatisfactory'. At its
meeting three days before, the cabinet had been informed that
prisoners from a German submarine, the U-39 sunk off the Hebrides,
had been found to possess Irish cigarettes which seemed to show that at
some stage they had landed in neutral Eire. It was agreed that, in his
meeting with de Valera, Maffey should make the fullest use of any
information resulting from the interrogation of the German sailors.

Maffey returned to Dublin on 20 September with the letter from
Chamberlain asking de Valera as a special favour to agree to the title
of British Representative in Ireland for Maffey. Chamberlain added
that this would be a compromise between the British and Irish points
of view. In fact it was not a compromise for the British who, as we
have seen, were determined to refuse a diplomatic title if the customary
'High Commissioner' was not acceptable. But de Valera studied the
proposed title for a few moments and, in a typical gesture, then
crossed out 'in' making it British Representative *to* Eire. On such
nuances does diplomacy thrive.

In his report Maffey reveals his shock at the deterioration in de
Valera's eyesight.[11] When he was given Chamberlain's letter, de Valera
was scarcely able to open the envelope and for several embarrassing
minutes he tried with little success to read the letter until Maffey tactfully
suggested that he read it for him. The Taoiseach's near-blindness at
such a critical stage in the country's affairs was not of course revealed
to the public but an operation a year later gave some improvement.

Following his instructions, Maffey brought up the question of coast-
watching and the possible intrusion by German submarines, but it is
interesting that in his detailed diary he makes no reference to the incident of the U-39 crew having Irish cigarettes, which would seem to
show that fuller interrogation had disproved the theory that German
sailors had been ashore in neutral Eire. As we shall see in the next
chapter, Churchill was only too anxious to exploit this incident in his
campaign to get back the ports. Maffey was able to reach an under-

standing with de Valera whereby the Irish coast-watching service would wireless any information it had about the movements of German submarines *en clair* and it would be up to the British Admiralty to pick it up. A similar arrangement about the movements of German aircraft was later made, but at British request the radio messages were made in code. Proposals by Maffey that Royal Navy officers and men of Irish origin might serve on the coast-watching service and that British aircraft that 'may occasionally land like exhausted birds on Irish shores' should be repatriated were accepted for consideration by de Valera, but neither proposal seems to have been ultimately accepted.

The question of British warships entering Irish territorial waters to attack German submarines which had infringed the neutrality rules was more delicate, and Maffey's suggestion that Eire should 'turn a blind eye' to such a British action may have had an appropriate Nelsonian ring but it was received in silence by de Valera and also Walshe. Maffey took this silence to be tacit acceptance. On his side, de Valera requested that the thousands of Irishmen who were deliberately permitted by the Irish government to serve in the British forces should wear civilian clothes when coming to Ireland on leave. The presence of large numbers of men in British uniforms in Irish streets could give rise to serious incidents, de Valera pointed out, and Maffey and later Eden found his request reasonable. As a result, dumps of civilian clothes were set up at Holyhead for Irish servicemen going home on leave and the system worked smoothly throughout the war.[12]

Before Maffey left his office, de Valera brought him over to the black map of Ireland with the white blemish on the north-east corner and said: 'There's the real source of all our trouble.' Maffey adds: 'He could not let me go without that.' Other foreign visitors to de Valera were also to be given the 'map treatment'. The British historian, Nicholas Bethell, sums up these meetings thus: 'Britain had won only a few concessions. The days were past when Britain could bully the Irish, and now the boot was on the other foot. It was Britain whose independence was threatened, and she was having to woo Ireland abjectly, from a position of weakness.'[13]

The country at large had little idea of whatever diplomatic success Mr de Valera might be achieving, and the war itself seemed remote and even unreal. The half-hearted attempt to blackout Dublin during the first week of the war was largely experimental and the effect was studied by army aircraft. When efforts were made to extend the blackout to country districts there were loud protests, and the fact that many pedestrians were mown down on pitch-black country roads by cars with candle-strength sidelights was raised in the Dail.

The call-up of about 10,000 reserves found the army seriously unprepared, and mothers complained to their TDs that their sons had not enough blankets and were underfed as the last meal was tea and bread in the late afternoon. The soldier who wanted to eat after that had to pay for it himself out of his meagre allowance, the size of which can be gauged from the fact that it cost the army just over £2 a week ($8) to pay *and* maintain a private, third class.

The first month of the war was one of wild rumours in Dublin and elsewhere. After the Emergency Powers debate at the beginning of the month, the Dail rose and for several weeks until it sat again, there was a persistent rumour that Mr Frank Aiken, the former Minister for Defence and now the Minister for the Co-ordination of Defensive Measures, was under arrest in Arbour Hill military prison. Another version was that both he and Mr de Valera had been executed! In fact, Mr Aiken was very busy setting up the press censorship system which was to be his main preoccupation for the rest of the war. The first directives issued to the Press forbade even the slightest discussion of the neutrality policy, any weather reports, movements by the defence forces or any reports which could prejudice economic or financial security. The censors interpreted the directives so strictly that humorous articles about the weather were censored as were quotations from speeches by de Valera himself on neutrality. This last was in the case of the Catholic weekly, *The Standard*, which was also anti-British and caused the government some embarrassment by implicitly questioning whether Irish neutrality was really as impartial towards both belligerents as had been publicly affirmed.

The attitude of the Catholic clergy in Ireland towards the war was very closely watched in London where it was assumed that clerical opinion was an accurate pointer to Irish public opinion generally, given the influence of the church. Thus it was reported to the Foreign Office that Sir Shane Leslie, a relation of Churchill and a well-known Irish author, had been visiting Cardinal McRory, the Primate of All-Ireland, in his residence in Armagh, Northern Ireland. The cardinal, a fiery northern nationalist, had complained to Leslie that being surrounded by Protestants he felt cut off from information and lacked contact with government authorities. It was suggested that the Ministry of Information in London should take on the job of keeping His Eminence informed.[14]

Another Anglo-Irish visitor who was advising London on how best to deal with neutral Ireland was Frank Pakenham, now Lord Longford. By October 1939 Pakenham had become aware of Churchill's pressure in the Admiralty and the war cabinet to take action over the Irish ports, and he wrote a long memorandum passed on to the Foreign Office which urged how disastrous this course would be on Irish opinion which was 80 per cent in favour of neutrality with a 'mild Allied preference'. Instead, Pakenham advised that the Irish government be given 'six fast anti-submarine craft' to permit them to exclude German U-boats from their waters.[15] In fact, London soon afterwards did start supplying Eire with the first of six motor torpedo boats which had been originally ordered by Estonia. But Pakenham's unease at 'the chance of the Admiralty doing anything rash' concerning the Irish ports was justified, and Churchill was having to be restrained by Chamberlain and Eden.

Notes to this chapter are on p 179

Chapter 2

The Ports

From the first day of the war the Treaty Ports, as they were known, became a contentious issue in Anglo-Irish relations increasingly involving the United States and even threatening at various critical times to lead to war between Britain and Ireland, strange as this may appear today. Ireland's refusal to hand over the ports to the allied cause was portrayed in the popular British press, and to a lesser extent in the American, as a stab in the back from a so-called friend at the hour of greatest need by causing the deaths of thousands of sailors bringing vital supplies across the Atlantic, not just to Britain, but even to neutral Eire. The bitterness felt as a result of this propaganda can be seen in the best-selling war novel, *The Cruel Sea*, where Nicholas Monsarrat describes the feelings aroused in wartime convoys as they passed the coastal lighting of unblacked-out Eire. The Northern Ireland poet, Louis MacNeice, expressed these feelings in his poem entitled 'Neutrality':

> But then look eastward from your heart, there bulks
> A continent, close, dark, as archetypal sin,
> While to the west off your own shores the mackerel
> Are fat – on the flesh of your kin.[1]

It is easy to understand British disappointment and even bitterness at the Irish refusal to hand over the ports when war broke out, but these feelings derived to a large extent from a misunderstanding of the historical background and from Churchill's own emotional attitude on the question which prevented him from viewing it in a rational manner. The essential background to the ports issue can be quickly told.

The Anglo-Irish Treaty of 6 December 1921 laid down in Article

Six that until the Irish Free State undertook her own coastal defence, 'the defence by sea of Great Britain and Ireland shall be undertaken by His Majesty's Imperial Forces'. Article Seven stated that the government of the Irish Free State shall afford to his Majesty's Imperial Forces:

> (a) In time of peace such harbour and other facilities as are indicated in the Annex hereto, or such facilities as may from time to time be agreed between the British Government and the Government of the Irish Free State; and (b) In time of war or of strained relations with a Foreign Power such harbour and other facilities as the British Government may require for the purposes of such defence aforesaid.

The facilities referred to were at Cobh (then known as Queenstown) in Cork Harbour on the south coast, Berehaven in Bantry Bay on the south-west and at Lough Swilly on the extreme north in Co Donegal. These had all been used by the Royal Navy during World War I, and the anti-submarine war had been largely conducted from Queenstown, but their main value was as deep-water anchorages and they were by no means fully equipped naval bases. By 1939 the shore installations were regarded as primitive and totally inadequate for a modern fleet. The coastal guns in the defensive batteries were in reasonable working order but rather old.

Up to 1938 small British military maintenance parties occupied the various forts, but in that year a new Anglo-Irish Agreement was concluded whereby the British government unconditionally handed over the forts and harbours to the Irish government thus abrogating Articles Six and Seven of the 1921 Treaty. The 1938 agreement also provided a financial settlement to the 'Economic War', which had broken out between the two countries when Mr de Valera's Government in 1932 withheld the payment of land annuities to Britain, and restored Irish trade with Britain to operating under the Imperial Preference System.

To get back possession of the Treaty Ports at a time when World War II was already looming over Europe was a tremendous coup on de Valera's part, so much so that many people both in Ireland and Britain were unable to believe that there were no strings attached. Although de Valera was deeply disappointed that no progress had been made in the 1938 negotiations in solving the partition issue, he was immensely grateful to Chamberlain for his co-operation in the restoration of the ports thereby enabling Ireland to have for the first time a

real neutrality policy. Churchill, on the other hand, never forgave
Chamberlain or Malcolm McDonald, the then Dominions Secretary,
for what he regarded as sheer folly. In his war memoirs more than ten
years after the event, his indignation was still seething:

> Personally I remain convinced that the gratuitous surrender of our right to
> use the Irish ports in war was a major injury to British national life and
> safety. A more feckless act can hardly be imagined – and at such a time. It is
> true that in the end we survived without the ports. It is also true that if we
> had not been able to do without them we should have retaken them by
> force rather than perish by famine. But this is no excuse. Many a ship and
> many a life were soon to be lost as the result of this improvident example
> of appeasement.[2]

Churchill also recalled how at the time of the 1921 Anglo-Irish
negotiations, Michael Collins, the IRA Adjutant-General, said to him:
'Of course you must have the ports. They are necessary for your life.'
It has also been pointed out that even when Mr de Valera violently
disagreed with the proposed treaty and drew up his own version known
as Document No 2, he still conceded the use of the ports to Britain.
According to Sir John Maffey in an interview with the *Irish Times* in
1962, the Irish High Commissioner in London, John Dulanty, 'could
hardly believe his own ears' when he heard the ports were being given
back, and Maffey went on to say that 'the blame for this incredible
miscalculation is entirely attributable to the British General Staff'.

Miscalculation or not, it is true that the decision to hand back the
ports was based on the recommendations of the Chiefs of Staff Sub-
committee (they had been asked for advice by the Minister for the
Co-ordination of Defence) consisting of Lord Chatfield for the navy,
C. L. Newall for the RAF and Lord Gort for the army.

On 12 January 1938 the Chiefs of Staff advised that 'the retention or
capture of the ports in the face of a hostile attitude on the part of Ireland would at best involve a most formidable military commitment
and might, even so, be impossible'.[3]

Churchill must have felt a wry satisfaction when the war cabinet at
its second meeting on 4 September was already stressing 'the importance of Berehaven' in the anti-submarine war. Churchill had just been
recalled to the cabinet as First Lord of the Admiralty and on the same
day he sent a memorandum to the First Sea Lord, Admiral Sir Dudley
Pound and others asking for a special report 'upon the questions

arising from the so-called neutrality of the so-called Eire'. He wanted to know what intelligence said about the 'possible succouring of U-Boats by Irish malcontents in West of Ireland inlets'. He also wanted a study on the addition to the radius of the destroyers through not having Berehaven and on the advantages of having the Irish bases. He admitted that satisfaction might not be obtained as 'Eirish neutrality raises political issues which have not yet been faced'.[4]

These political issues had become somewhat clearer following the two visits to Dublin of Sir John Maffey described in the last chapter, but there was little joy there for Mr Churchill who on 24 September was updating his instructions for Admiralty dealings with 'Southern Ireland':

> All this talk about partition and the bitterness that would be healed by a union of Northern and Southern Ireland will amount to nothing. They will not unite at the present time and we cannot in any circumstances sell the loyalists of Northern Ireland . . .
>
> There seems to be a good deal of evidence, or at any rate, suspicion that the U-Boats are being succoured from West of Ireland ports by the malignant section with whom de Valera dare not interfere. [In fact, the internment of sixty-four republicans had been announced the day before.] If the U-Boat campaign becomes more dangerous we should coerce Southern Ireland both about coast watching and the use of Berehaven etc.

Three weeks later the Deputy Chief of Naval Staff told the war cabinet that the lack of Berehaven was a serious hindrance in the anti-submarine warfare. He said it would be a big help if the navy was even allowed to put a tug there and 'it might prove to be the thin end of the wedge'.[5] But the real pressure came following the shock sinking of the battleship *Royal Oak* by a German submarine at Scapa Flow. Two days later on 17 October Churchill told the cabinet that the fleet must have alternative harbours and he referred to Lough Swilly and Berehaven. He stressed the usefulness of the first as German aircraft would have to cross Britain to attack it. He said bluntly: 'The time has come to make it clear to the Eire Government that we must have the use of these harbours and intend in any case to use them.' Eden is recorded as demurring but the cabinet agreed that it was of the utmost importance to get Lough Swilly and Berehaven, and Eden was asked to advise on the best way of doing so. Churchill was asked to formulate his reasons.

Churchill had in fact overplayed his hand in his obsession with the ports, and the next day he had to admit to the cabinet that he had perhaps overstated the case for wanting the Irish ports as an alternative to Scapa Flow since there were other anchorages available. But he repeated the demand for Berehaven claiming it could be used by battleships on escort duties which at present had to be escorted themselves from Milford Haven. He hoped Eden would persuade de Valera to meet British needs over Berehaven as soon as possible. Eden, who knew the task was well nigh hopeless, said he had recalled Maffey for talks on it and he thought the most useful approach would be to show that they wanted Berehaven to combat the U-boat menace from which the Eire trade would also suffer.[6]

Maffey was given careful instructions for the vital interview, based mainly on a memorandum from the naval staff, on the importance of Berehaven in the anti-submarine campaign as it would give destroyers and seaplanes patrolling the south-west approaches an extra 400 miles range. On the political side, the instructions said that it was fully appreciated that the 1938 agreement transferring the ports was 'unconditional' but

> There is nothing in the agreement to prevent the Government of Eire from according facilities to vessels of the Royal Navy to make use of the Eire ports. The United Kingdom Government have always felt and have indeed made it clear to the Government of Eire before and at the time of the 1938 discussions that in their view in a state of emergency circumstances might arise which rendered it imperative, in the interests of both countries, that such facilities should be accorded. These circumstances have now arisen.[7]

It was a brave try but there should have been no illusions about de Valera's attitude. For him the 1938 agreement had only been a partial success as the partition problem remained unsolved and any British mental reservations about the transfer of the ports would cut no ice. In an interview with the *Evening Standard* six months after the agreement on 17 October 1938, de Valera was asked about the possibility of co-operation in defence with Britain if there were a united Ireland. He answered cautiously that in those circumstances some form of association with the British Commonwealth would be maintained and that it would be 'possible to visualise a critical situation arising in the future in which a united Ireland would be willing to co-operate with Britain to resist a common attack'. But, he continued, 'the chances of such a co-operation in the event of a European war are very slight while Partition remains. If such a war occurred while British forces were in occupation of any part of Ireland, Irish sentiment would definitely be hostile to any co-operation.' It might be added that whether British forces remained in the north or not, de Valera was fairly determined to follow a neutral course as he indicated in a speech at the League of Nations in June 1936 when the collective security myth was finally shattered by the shelving of the economic sanctions policy against Italy over the annexation of Abyssinia. Reading the signs, de Valera declared, 'All the small states can do, if the statesmen of the greater states fail in their duty, is resolutely to determine that they will not become the tools of any Great Power, and that they will resist with whatever strength they may possess every attempt to force them into a war against their will.'[8] A short time afterwards, reporting the failure of sanctions to the Dail, de Valera was even more explicit: 'The small states in Europe have begun to provide for their own defences . . . we must be neutral.'[9]

When Maffey went to see de Valera, therefore, on 21 October 1939, with a request which if granted was the equivalent of a declaration of war on Germany, he was dealing with a man who had made up his mind three years before to keep Ireland neutral and however much he might regret the partition of the country it was a most useful argument with which to counter British pleas and veiled threats. Maffey reported the ninety-minute talk at length for the benefit of Eden and the cabinet, and the unwavering stance of de Valera must have impressed them as much as it did Maffey.[10] He reported de Valera as saying:

> The creed of Ireland today was neutrality. No Government could exist that departed from that principle. The question of the ports was at the very nerve centre of public interest in that matter, and the public mood would react with intense violence to any action invalidating their integrity. If a demand were made – he fully realised that no demand was being made – he would be forced at whatever cost to treat such a situation as a challenge and his Parliament would endorse his measures. If, on the other hand, facilities were voluntarily afforded in breach of neutrality, his Government could not live. No other Government which might endeavour to meet our request could survive for twenty-four hours.

De Valera said that if Britain had paved the way to Irish unity, Ireland 'might' have been able to co-operate with them. His sympathies were with the allies and he would greatly regret a German victory but if there was a 'vague majority sentiment' in favour of the allies, there would be a swift change of opinion following any assault on Irish interests. There were many people in Ireland, he said, ready enough to acclaim a British defeat at any price. That view might be based on ignorance but it had its roots in history.

Maffey tried the moral approach on the ports. 'The path of generosity had been followed as an act of faith and in the belief that in the hour of need the hand of friendship would be extended.' De Valera countered by saying Britain had no right to derive advantage from what was not hers. 'Such a view,' he continued with unwitting irony, 'would justify encroachment by Germany on Holland or Belgium.' He went on to say that he found himself in complete agreement with everything Chamberlain had done in Europe. 'England has a moral position today,' he added. 'Hitler might have his early successes, but the moral position would tell.'

Maffey found that the interview only too clearly confirmed what his short stay in the country had taught him. In a letter to Eden two days later he wrote: 'The policy of neutrality commands widespread approval among all classes and interests in Eire. It is remarkable how even the "pro-British" group, men who have fought for the Crown and are anxious to be called up again, men whose sons are at the front today, loyalists in the old sense of the word, agree generally in supporting the policy of neutrality for Eire.'

There was a 'credit side' to this largely unfruitful approach for the ports and Maffey listed seven examples of rather unneutral co-operation. One was the exclusion from instructions to coastal organisations of any mention of British aircraft. 'Today our aircraft are flying over the headlands of Eire and even inland and nothing is being said.' (The main concessions here seemed to have been for the flying boats based at Lower Lough Erne to fly direct to the coast over part of Co Donegal, and for the planes at Co Derry airfields to fly over the Inishowen peninsula when on north Atlantic patrol.)

The rejection by de Valera of Maffey's request for the ports was discussed by the war cabinet on 24 October.

Churchill was not in a mood to take the rebuff lying down. In his view Ireland's neutrality was illegal. The king was still the Irish head of state and Germany was the king's enemy. It was improper for Ireland to remain neutral towards Germany and still more improper for her to

maintain diplomatic relations with Germany. The Irish envoy appointed to Berlin had had his letters of credence signed by the king. It was
wrong for the king to be represented in an enemy country. (In fact the
Irish minister to Berlin, Mr Bewley, noted for pro-German sympathies,
had been withdrawn just before the war but the man nominated as the
new Irish minister to Germany, Dr Kiernan, was unable to take up his
post as the king could hardly be expected to sign his letters of credence
accrediting him to an enemy country. The young First Secretary in
Berlin, Mr William Warnock, had to be promoted a chargé d'affaires
and he had the onerous duty of carrying on alone in the German
capital until the closing stages of the war, surviving the bombing of the
legation building in the Tiergarten district in November 1943 and
moving shop to a stud farm outside the city owned by an Irishman.)

Churchill's outburst did not end there. He suggested ominously that
the cabinet 'should take stock of the weapons of coercion'. At present
Eire had the best of both worlds – trade preferences, free access to
Britain and military and naval protection. She should be told she was at
the 'parting of the ways' and what she stood to lose by being declared
a foreign power. The law officers of the crown should examine the
constitutional position. If it were shown that Irish neutrality was illegal,
Britain should make this fact known to the world and could then 'insist
on the use of the ports'.

The cabinet clearly did not follow Churchill's imperialistic logic, but
Chamberlain humoured him by saying he had presented a 'powerful
case'. However, this was not yet established and it was difficult to say
now that the ports were a question of life and death. De Valera's
neutral attitude had been expected and he did not doubt his claim that
no government could survive which departed from it. The United
Kingdom should try and enlist the support of the dominions for getting
the ports, but he advised against their seizure because of repercussions
in the USA and India. It was hardly a very worthy motive for restraint
but the First Lord was in a difficult mood and the main aim was doubtless to calm him. The cabinet agreed to ask the Lord Chancellor to
prepare a memorandum on the legal and constitutional issues of ending
Eire's Commonwealth membership, and asked Eden to prepare one on
the financial, political and economic considerations involved.

These reports were duly drawn up and circulated to the cabinet and
they showed in no uncertain terms the disadvantages and risks of

expelling Ireland from the Commonwealth from every aspect.[11] One report concluded: 'It seems very doubtful whether any pressure which we could bring to bear upon Eire . . . would, in fact, induce the Government of Eire to accord us the facilities desired, while a breach with Eire would result in the loss of such cooperation, whatever it may be worth, as the Government of Eire are at present disposed to accord.'

Churchill's reaction to these conclusions is not recorded but a year later as prime minister he was to ignore this advice and deliberately embark on an economic pressure campaign in a vain hope of securing the Irish ports. But the Admiralty in November 1939 did its best to keep their irascible master happy and the Chief of the Naval Staff told the cabinet on 1 November that there were now a number of British agents in Ireland and a trawler was watching the coast. A naval attaché would be going to Dublin soon.

This trawler was probably the Q-boat called the *Tamura*, an unarmed trawler commanded by Captain W. R. Fell, which from September 1939 until March 1940 patrolled the west coast of Ireland, sometimes towing a submarine and acting as a decoy for U-boats which Churchill was convinced were lurking in the bays and inlets of Cork, Kerry, Galway and Mayo and were being refuelled and serviced by the 'malignant minority', most of whom were safely interned in the

Identification of people in photographs on facing page
(*Above*) *Front row*: Mr Eamon de Valera (Taoiseach); Colonel S. Brennan, ADC. *Second row: from left*: Mr Thomas Derrig (Minister for Education); Mr Sean Lemass (Minister for Supplies); Mr Sean MacEntee (Minister for Industry and Commerce); Mr Gerald Boland (Minister for Justice); Dr James Ryan (Minister for Agriculture); Mr Patrick Little (Minister for Posts and Telegraphs); Mr Oscar Traynor (Minister for Defence). *Third row*: Lt-General Daniel McKenna (Chief of Staff). *Fourth row*: Maj-General Hugo MacNeill (O/C Second Division); next officer not identified; Maj-General Liam Egan (Quartermaster-General); Colonel Liam Archer (Adjutant-General).

(*Below*) *Left to right* (*standing*): Sir Edward Bridges (Secretary to the War Cabinet); Mr Anthony Eden (Secretary of State for Dominion Affairs); Sir Kingsley Wood (Secretary of State for Air); Mr Winston Churchill (First Lord of the Admiralty); Mr Leslie Hore-Belisha (Secretary of State for War); Lord Hankey (Minister without Portfolio); Sir John Anderson (Minister for Home Security). (*Seated*): Lord Chatfield (Minister for the Co-ordination of Defence); Sir Samuel Hoare (Lord Privy Seal); Mr Neville Chamberlain (Prime Minister); Sir John Simon (Chancellor of the Exchequer); Viscount Halifax (Secretary of State for Foreign Affairs).

Page 33 (above) *Mr de Valera and his ministers taking the salute during a wartime Easter parade before the historic General Post Office building in O'Connell Street, Dublin;* (below) *the first picture taken of the British war cabinet in November 1939. See facing page for identifications.*

Page 34 (above left) *Sir John Maffey, appointed British representative to Ireland in October 1939;* (above right) *Dr Edouard Hempel, German minister to Ireland from 1937 to 1945;* (below left) *Mr David Gray, US minister to Ireland, appointed in February 1940;* (below right) *Signor Vincenzo Berardis, Italian minister to Ireland during the war years.*

Curragh military camp. Captain Fell describes his Irish adventure in *The Sea Our Shield* and says that they never saw or heard of a U-boat in Irish bays. There was possibly a second trawler being used, as Donald McLachlan in his book on naval intelligence, *Room 39*, also refers to a trawler fitted out 'to poke around the western ports of Ireland to report enemy activities'. He adds that 'the skipper was as credulous as he was adventurous and went ashore after an alleged spy ring, only to be arrested by the police who courteously released him through the British Representative in Dublin'. This certainly does not sound like Captain Fell, a brilliant officer who later developed one-man submarines for the navy.

As well as the Admiralty having its own 'agents' in Ireland for U-boat spotting, Lord Hankey, Minister without Portfolio, had been given the task of setting up an 'Intelligence Organisation' there and his proposals were approved on 20 December 1939. All the cabinet documents referring to this counter-espionage network of MI5 agents in Ireland have been closed to the public until 1990 and in some cases for 100 years. Various indiscreet references scattered throughout the files show that MI5's liaison man in London with the Irish operation was Cecil Liddell, Box No 500, Parliament Street BO, SW1 and he was occasionally listed as attending inter-ministerial meetings on Irish affairs. His brother, Captain Guy Liddell, who had Irish connections by marriage was also in MI5 and they both visited Dublin frequently and were on very friendly terms with the Irish army staff and used to visit some of the Dublin barracks. It seems ironic that in 1973 a sensation was caused first by the conviction of an Irish detective and a British intelligence agent for breaches of the Official Secrets Act; and secondly by the 'Littlejohn affair' in which a British bank robber was being used as a part-time agent in Ireland by the British intelligence services. A few British intelligence agents, who were acting without proper authorisation or who had become too indiscreet, were arrested, in 1939–40, also in Ireland, but without any publicity and they were eventually handed back to their superiors.

Needless to say, the average Irish citizen was totally unaware of British pressure for the ports and espionage activities. The Press censorship system operated by Mr Frank Aiken in his new capacity as Minister for the Co-ordination of Defensive Measures was so thorough as to be ruthless and the voluntary newspaper censorship, like the one

C

used in Britain throughout the war, was soon dropped in Ireland where the papers had to submit proofs of news matter to be passed before publication. War news was supplied by the main news agencies, British, American and German and took up most of the news pages but not a breath of critical comment concerning any of the belligerents was allowed in editorials except for pungent attacks on godless Russia for attacking Catholic Poland and little Finland. As with other mainly Catholic countries at the time, Stalin and atheistic communism aroused far more dread and revulsion in Ireland than did Hitler and the racist nazis.

On 11 September 'moving scenes' had been reported at the docks in Dublin as forty-two able-bodied males from the 400-strong German colony in Ireland sailed for home to fight for the fatherland. Dr Hempel and the other members of the German legation were there to see them off and Frau Hempel distributed roses. The departing group included scientists, academics and administrators in important positions in Irish life and the German Foreign Office. Abwehr, the secret service branch of the Wehrmacht, was later to regret that these influential men were not left in Ireland where they could have done more to help the German cause than in uniform on the eastern front. The Irish papers reported that the forty-two were leaving voluntarily but they had, in fact, been ordered to return to the Reich for military service although doubtless some of them would have done so anyhow.

Hempel was a shrewd and well-informed observer of the Irish scene. A tall handsome man of fifty-two, he had been born in Saxony and served as an officer in World War I. He entered the foreign service in 1927 with a doctorate in law and had served in numerous posts abroad, including India, the Far East and Norway before coming to Dublin in 1937. He was not then a member of the Nazi party and he told an Irish journalist in an interview after his retirement that the Irish government had indicated it did not want a party member as a German minister in Dublin. Later in the war Hempel did join the party and wore the badge in his lapel, but this was following the instruction to all non-nazi diplomats to join the party or leave the service. The number two at the legation in the semi-detached, red-brick house at 58 Northumberland Road in the southern suburbs was Henning Thomsen who has been portrayed in articles about the period as a fanatical young nazi who carried on cloak-and-dagger operations with the IRA and

German spies unknown to Hempel. This is most unlikely. There were only four diplomats in the legation and Hempel and Thomsen, the latter told the author, had four or five hours discussion every day on what they had learned and they drafted the telegrams to the Foreign Office on the Wilhelmstrasse together, so scope for independent action by Thomsen was extremely limited. After the war when Hempel had retired from the restored West German foreign service but Thomsen was still an ambassador, Hempel caused considerable embarrassment by saying that Thomsen had been a member of the SS when in Dublin. This was correct but not as sinister as it sounded.

Thomsen's own explanation is that when he was joining the foreign service before the war he was told by the Department of Personnel that not being a party member he would have no chance of being accepted as an attaché unless he joined either the SA or the SS. Hoping to avoid party membership altogether, he and all his comrades at the riding school at the Brandenburg Gate joined the Reiter SS (mounted SS) of which more than 90 per cent were not party members. They were kept apart from the rest of the SS and were used as escorts for foreign diplomats at formal occasions like Hindenburg's funeral.

On 7 October 1939, a few days after Sir John Maffey arrived officially in Dublin, Hempel sent back to Berlin an assessment of the political situation.[12] He said that neutrality had the support of the vast majority of the population 'despite the undermining effect of certain pro-British circles'. The Irish army was supposedly ready to defend neutrality in all directions in spite of the presence of pro-British elements. The IRA was quiet. He reported 'anti-German feeling' following the pact with Russia and the fate of Poland, but there was also strong anti-British feeling. In spite of Poland, the Catholic Church was obeying the government's appeal for a neutral stand, and the attitude of the government to Hempel personally was 'definitely friendly'. Consequently he advised that Germany should continue to support the consolidation of Irish neutrality and independence on a broad basis as it was a 'symptom of the loosening ties of the Empire' and could have important effects on the other dominions and in India and America. It was, after all, quite an achievement for German diplomacy for one of the countries of the British Commonwealth headed by the king to remain neutral, and German diplomacy right through the war worked for the continuance of this state of affairs.

But the IRA and their active hostility to Britain could not be
ignored by Germany. Berlin would be continually divided on whether
or not to cash in on IRA militancy, especially in sabotage operations in
Northern Ireland. This would have risked a diplomatic breach with de
Valera, who saw Irish neutrality depending on his subjugating the IRA
in fulfilment of his pledge not to allow Irish territory to be used as a
base to attack Britain. In a memo to Ribbentrop, the Reich Foreign
Minister, in February 1940, Under State Secretary Woermann, who
handled Irish affairs in the Foreign Office, explained that the Irish
government and the IRA both sought Irish unity but differed in the
means. By reason of its militant attitude to England, the IRA was 'the
natural ally of Germany'.[13] This schizophrenic attitude of Berlin towards Ireland was to be Hempel's biggest worry, but his continual
urging that the IRA should not be tampered with as it was a thoroughly
unreliable body was in the main successful.

Rumours in Dublin of undercover connections between German
intelligence agents and the IRA were increasing towards the end of
1939, and on 13 November Hempel advised Berlin to exercise 'complete restraint'. The IRA was not strong enough for success and had no
leader of stature. The more level-headed republican elements were
against an open line-up with Germany as they realised the popular
backing for neutrality.

Hempel went on to be more explicit about the 'Irish Cause' saying:
'I have heard the hope expressed – probably felt in some Government
circles although hardly by de Valera so far – that at a suitable time we
would promise Ireland our support for the return of Northern
Ireland, to be made good at the conclusion of peace and thereby assure
ourselves the friendship of all Irishmen.' Hempel added that he did not
think that the time for this had yet arrived. But the Irish unity card was
to be one which both the British and the Germans were to keep up
their sleeves for a more appropriate occasion. For both sides the
occasion was to come during the critical events of 1940 when, para-
doxically, the British feared a German invasion of Ireland as a back-
door into Britain and the Germans feared the forcible seizure of the
Irish ports by a Churchill infuriated by the appalling shipping losses in
the Atlantic.

Notes to this chapter are on pp 179–80

Chapter 3

Britain Plays the Unity Card

The year 1940 opened with the Irish government still shocked by
a daring IRA coup. Two days before Christmas the IRA had raided
the magazine fort in the Phoenix Park, west of Dublin, overcome the
small garrison and coolly got away with over one million rounds of
ammunition in thirteen lorries. Several weeks earlier the government
had received an embarrassing setback in its attempts to deal with the
IRA when the internment of republicans under the Offences Against
the State Act of June 1939 was declared unconstitutional and fifty-three
of them were released. The government reacted vigorously. Within
days large caches of the stolen ammunition were being recovered. An
IRA transmitter being used for attempts at spasmodic communication
with the Abwehr and internal propaganda was seized in Dublin, and
the Emergency Powers Act, which transcended all constitutional rights,
was amended to allow the internment of Irish citizens as well as aliens.

This unease on the domestic front fell into perspective with the
lightning German invasion of Norway and Denmark in the first weeks
of April 1940 and guarded criticism of the German action was expressed
in the *Irish Press*. The invasion of Holland and Belgium and the sudden
vulnerability of France in May naturally increased apprehension in
Ireland where the value of official neutrality where Hitler was concerned was seen as highly dubious. Maffey hoped to exploit this mood
and called on de Valera without waiting for instruction from London
on 10 May.[1]

He told de Valera that it was obvious that these new aggressions by

Germany made it necessary for him to reconsider his position in relation to the allied cause. It was indeed a fateful moment in the history of his country, and Maffey trusted that Britian would find Ireland in her natural place 'namely, no longer neutral in the cause of freedom'. But as Maffey expected, de Valera immediately reached for the inevitable counter-argument of partition. Maffey's report continued:

> This talk on Partition ran its normal course and I will not repeat the arguments and counter-arguments for they are stale . . . I said 'If the Partition question were solved today would you automatically be our active Ally?' He replied 'I feel convinced that that would probably be the consequence.' I said that the question was obviously only an academic one as in wartime no attention could be given to the solution of such questions.

But the question was not as academic as Maffey believed and Churchill, who had become prime minister that same day, was to reopen it the following month using Chamberlain and Malcolm MacDonald as intermediaries because of their friendship with de Valera.

Maffey then proceeded to lecture de Valera telling him that his view on a grave crisis in world affairs was from too narrow an angle. Here was a maniacal force let loose in the world. It was not a time to talk of Anglo-Irish disputes which in the fullness of time would be peacefully resolved. Where did Ireland stand? Why not send an Irish brigade to France? Surely the soul of Ireland would be stirred, and so forth. 'But we always travelled back to the old prejudice, to Partition, to the bitterness in the hearts of the active and extremist elements. I suggested that with clear leadership the adventurous spirits would respond to a better call. But Mr de Valera held to his narrow view. He seems incapable of courageous or original thought and now on this world issue and in every matter he lives too much under the threat of the extremist.'

Doubtless the emotion aroused in Maffey by the alarming turn of events on the Western Front contributed to his deep disillusionment with de Valera at this point and explains this exceptional outburst. The charge of surrender to extremism is at odds with Maffey's own assessment of the Irish situation following his interview with de Valera in October 1939 about the ports and quoted in the previous chapter. It also ignores the fact that a few weeks earlier de Valera had taken the difficult decision to let two IRA men on hunger strike, Darcy and McNeela, starve to death in prison.

The uncomfortable interview ended with de Valera reminding Maffey that repeated Irish requests to buy British arms had not been answered (some motor torpedo boats had been delivered, however) and refusing to take the hint that the German legation should be closed to remove the danger of a Quisling-style infiltration. He also had a few words of consolation for the disturbed Maffey who with uncharacteristically bad syntax, reports them thus: 'Before I left he said that patience was necessary, things would move slowly but that they might move in time. People would learn to realise what a German triumph would mean. He was making a speech tomorrow in Galway and would see what could be said on that subject.'

In the Galway speech de Valera sympathised publicly with Belgium and Holland saying: 'Today, these two small nations are fighting for their lives and I think I would be unworthy of this small nation if, on an occasion like this, I did not utter our protest against the cruel wrong that has been done them.' But an all-conquering Germany was in no mood to accept moral rebukes and Hempel was ordered by Berlin to protest at de Valera's speech.

A week later Abbeville, near the Channel coast, fell to the Germans and de Valera and his advisers were thoroughly alarmed about the likelihood of a German descent on Ireland. The next day, 22 May, there was something like panic in government circles in Dublin when the police raided a house in the suburb of Templeogue belonging to an Irish businessman of German parentage, Stephen Carroll Held, and found recent traces of the presence of a German parachutist, a file containing military details about Irish harbours, airfields, bridges, roads and landing places and about the distribution of the Irish defence forces. There was also a wireless transmitter and receiver, a code book and a safe with about $20,000.[2] Only a few days previously Chamberlain had written to de Valera warning him to 'consider very seriously the danger of enemy landings from troop-carrying planes. The Germans do not respect neutrality and the rapidity and efficiency of their methods are terrifying.'[3] The combination of events shocked de Valera into drastic action and Joe Walshe, the Head of the Department of External Affairs, was despatched immediately to London on a top-secret mission along with Colonel Liam Archer, head of the G2 military intelligence section of army headquarters.

The Chiefs of Staff committee on Eire has recorded in a memorandum dated 30 May 1940 that on 23 May de Valera gave the following messages to the Dominions Secretary:[4] (a) there was no question that Eire would fight if attacked by Germany and would call in assistance from the United Kingdom the moment it became necessary; (b) the political situation was such that there was no question of inviting in United Kingdom troops *before* the actual descent and before fighting had begun. If United Kingdom troops arrived before this, he could not be responsible for the political consequences; (c) he did not feel any danger from local fifth columnists etc. All suspects in Eire were under watch and he was satisfied with the control.

Mr de Valera, the report continued, had suggested that 'immediate secret contacts should be established between the Irish military authorities and the service staffs in this country with a view to concerting the military action which would be taken when the occasion arises'. This offer had been accepted and secret talks had taken place and were continuing.

The Irish government had been told that when the call for assistance came 'they may expect to receive direct support as far as land forces are concerned from General Officer Commanding Northern Ireland district. Staff officers from headquarters, Northern Ireland, have attended the conversations in Dublin and detailed planning is now proceeding. There have also been talks on how the R.A.F. can help from United Kingdom bases.' Since very early information on the German invasion of Eire was essential and the cable would probably be cut, the report went on, arrangements were in hand by the War Office and the Air Ministry to supplement existing communications and Maffey was to get a special wireless set. To increase the liaison the Chiefs of Staff proposed, subject to de Valera's approval, sending military and air attachés to Dublin but in view of secrecy the appointments would probably have to be 'camouflaged'. The war cabinet was asked to approve of the foregoing, especially the principle that military support should be provided if called for. The cabinet gave its approval on 1 June 1940.

Behind this soberly phrased report lay a curious episode, the full story of which has never been told lest it embarrass the Irish government.

On 24 May, Walshe of External Affairs and Colonel Liam Archer, Director of Military Intelligence, were despatched to London on a top-secret mission known only to de Valera, several members of the government and the most senior staff officers. The two emissaries had the embarrassing task for Irishmen of seeking British military help in the event of a German invasion. A young staff officer, Lt-Colonel Dudley Clarke, who had just returned from Norway where he had observed the German *blitzkrieg* first-hand was assigned by the War Office to co-ordinate Anglo-Irish defence measures, and that same day he flew to Belfast in the twin-engined Flamingo aircraft used by Churchill bringing Walshe and Archer with him. They insisted that he travel in mufti and look as little like a British officer as possible.

The next day Clarke travelled to Dublin by train, his two companions having gone on ahead. In the afternoon Walshe collected Clarke at the Shelbourne Hotel in his own car and after driving around for some time brought him to what looked to Clarke like 'an engineer's dump for the Public Works department', then down some steps, along underground corridors and finally into a conference room where members of the army staff were waiting in civilian clothes. The rendezvous in Government Buildings was, if Clarke had only known it, about three minutes from the hotel but Walshe was revelling in the cloak-and-dagger atmosphere.

Clarke, who was not introduced to any of the officers present (he never even knew Walshe's name and presumed he was a cabinet minister), told them that General Huddleston, the GOC Northern Ireland, had a mobile column waiting across the border for the signal to come down and help the Irish army against the Germans. The Irish officers drew up a list of the weapons and equipment they needed.

The next morning Clarke was examining some curios in the National Museum as instructed, when Walshe suddenly appeared at his side and drew him into the curator's store and back into the twisting passages. On the way Walshe invited Clarke to have a quick look at the Dail chamber under which they were passing and he was suitably impressed. The conference this time was attended by the Chief of Staff, General McKenna, who made it absolutely clear to Clarke that there was no question of calling for British aid until the German invasion had started and the Irish government gave the go-ahead. This was a big setback for Clarke who had been instructed to try at all costs to get British troops into Eire beforehand, but since he could not budge McKenna they passed on to discussing the military co-operation on this basis. It was agreed that a British military attaché would be appointed to Dublin for liaison purposes but in the guise of a civilian.

That night Clarke dined with Frank Aiken although he only knew him as the 'Minister of Defence'. Walshe warned him that as the minister's support would be necessary for the staff liaison plans he 'should pay due respect to his personal notions for the better conduct of the war in general'. This for Clarke meant spending a bemused evening listening to Aiken, 'the most enthusiastic of amateur inventors', expounding 'a dozen new ideas for the mechanical improvement of the War'. Walshe also enlisted Clarke for a tour of the Phoenix Park so that he could advise on how best to guard it against German paratroop landings. He also arranged a picnic for Clarke on the hills overlooking Baldonnel military airfield for the same purpose, but a solitary cyclist so alarmed Walshe that he snatched the field-glasses from Clarke's hands and rushed him back to the Shelbourne.

In spite of the bizarre aspects of his visit, Clarke left feeling that a satisfactory arrangement had been made for defence co-ordination if the worst came to the worst. The biggest surprise of all came in 1947 when he wrote about his Dublin visit in his book *Seven Assignments* only to be ordered under the Official Secrets Act to strike out all reference to what country the episode had taken place in and this he had to do. Dublin and London co-operated closely whenever it was a question of suppressing information.[5]

Throughout the second half of May and early June the war cabinet had been receiving a succession of reports of an impending German invasion of Ireland and of the unpreparedness of the Irish army to put up more than token resistance. On 27 May the cabinet asked Chamberlain and Eden, now Secretary of State for War, to approach de Valera about the use of Berehaven and the need for co-operation and to sound out Lord Craigavon, Prime Minister of Northern Ireland, about the setting up of a Council of Defence for the whole of Ireland. On 30 May Chamberlain, who had now become dangerously obsessed with the Irish question, told the cabinet that the IRA was now strong enough to overrun the Eire defence forces, a ludicrous view which shows the state of mind he had reached. The next day he was again expressing his fears of a German invasion of Eire, and on 3 June the cabinet heard a report that Germans were assembling at Cadiz for the invasion of Ireland and that de Valera had already been informed. Restrictions on unnecessary travel between Eire and Britain were now introduced and led to demonstrations by seasonal agricultural workers outside the British permit office in Dublin and action was urgently needed to calm them down.

On 16 June with France tottering before the final collapse, the war cabinet held a long and detailed meeting on Ireland. Chamberlain said he had recently received a report from Sir Charles Tegart which gave a very alarming picture of German preparations in Southern Ireland (these existed only in the imaginations of some amateur agents), and made it clear that a body of some 2,000 German troops could probably capture the whole country. He had, therefore, written to Mr de Valera referring to this information which made it clear that Ireland was in grave peril. He had suggested that personal conversations between himself and Mr de Valera were now vitally important and had invited him to come to London for that purpose but de Valera had since refused.

He had seen Lord Craigavon some ten days before, Chamberlain went on, and had pointed out to him how difficult it would be to separate questions of defence from the burning question of partition, and had invited him to consider what conciliatory gesture the people of Northern Ireland would be prepared to make. Lord Craigavon had said that he would seriously consider this matter but so far no reply from him had been received. Chamberlain said he had therefore decided to ask Mr Malcolm MacDonald, the Minister of Health, to go to Dublin. He might hope to pass unrecognised and was on very friendly terms with Mr de Valera. MacDonald was to go over the next day and he had explained the matter very fully to him. It was most important that Mr de Valera should be told frankly of the arrangements that the Germans had made (the indefatigable Sir Charles Tegart would supply them). He must realise that it would be too late to do anything after the invasion had started, when bridges would be blown up to impede troop movements and Mr de Valera himself probably shot (the British themselves nearly managed it in 1916). The whole thing might be over in a matter of hours. Adequate defence preparations must be taken beforehand. They should like Mr de Valera to throw neutrality aside and invite British troops to assist in the defence of Ireland; but they could hardly hope to get his agreement to this. Mr MacDonald should, however, insist on the rounding up of the IRA and the internment of Germans. If this precipitated a rebellion, as it well might, so much the better. The Eire army would then be fighting the IRA and upsetting the German arrangements.

At some time during the interview Mr de Valera would be sure to raise the question of partition. When he did, MacDonald would suggest that a council for the defence of all-Ireland should be set up, which would not only consider matters of defence, but would form a bridge for eventual discussions on partition. If Mr de Valera could be persuaded to accept this proposition, then Mr MacDonald was to go on and see Lord Craigavon and persuade him to accept it also.

Churchill welcomed Mr MacDonald's proposed visit to Mr de Valera and agreed that, although as a last resort they should not hesitate to secure the ports by force, it would be unwise at this moment to take any action that might compromise their position with the USA in view of the present delicate developments. (He does not seem to have mentioned that he had already written twice to President Roosevelt asking him to send a US naval squadron on a prolonged visit to Irish ports as a deterrent to a German invasion. Roosevelt refused the request saying a squadron could not be spared but according to the American historians, Langer and Gleason, the real reason was Roosevelt's fear of being accused by the Irish-Americans in an election year of pressing Eire to abandon neutrality.)[6]

Carefully coached by Chamberlain on the lines indicated above, Malcolm MacDonald, who was a son of the former Labour Prime Minister, Ramsay MacDonald, flew to Dublin and had a three and a half hour meeting with de Valera. The day before, Sunday, 16 June, de Valera had addressed an enormous crowd in College Green as the climax of the nationwide recruiting drive launched at the end of May. With him on the platform set up in front of the historic Bank of Ireland building which had housed the last all-Ireland parliament at the end of the eighteenth century, were the leaders of the two opposition parties, Mr W. T. Cosgrave of Fine Gael and Mr W. Norton of Labour. The opposition parties had also agreed three weeks previously to participate with Fianna Fail in a defence conference with an advisory voice in 'matters of national defence'. The recruiting rally was an impressive and public show of national unity at a critical time and de Valera, who only twenty years before had been hunted and imprisoned as a rebel by Mr Cosgrave's Government, must have felt a special gratification at this visible sign of the healing of old wounds in face of the common danger.

He was, therefore, in no mood for concessions from internal weakness when he met MacDonald. The latter gave a detailed report to the war cabinet on 20 June showing that he had faithfully followed Chamberlain's instructions. He began by stressing the danger of a German invasion and how it might become an 'effective occupation of the Twenty-six Counties within a few hours from landing'. The arrival of British military aid from Northern Ireland might well be hindered by sabotage of road and rail communication by the IRA or German fifth columnists. The wisest course for Eire would be the immediate abandonment of her neutrality and complete co-operation with Britain in resistance to Germany. 'To this suggestion Mr. de Valera had returned an emphatic negative. He said the whole force of public opinion was against any abandonment of neutrality a moment before it was inevitable.'

MacDonald had been told to anticipate this refusal, so he passed on to the next proposal. Would it be possible for the Eire government, with the support of the opposition, to invite British warships to use Irish ports and to call in British troops to guard strategic points? Again de Valera refused pointing out that 'the national unity which had been achieved between the various parties in the country was based on the continued maintenance of the policy of neutrality and on the firm resistance to the forces of either belligerent who became the aggressor'. (In a fortnight's time Fine Gael were to put out feelers to de Valera about the abandonment of neutrality. If they had done so earlier, de Valera would not have faced MacDonald on this and his two subsequent visits with such confidence in his internal position.)[7]

To emphasise his resoluteness, de Valera added that it would make no difference to his answer whether the forces which came in were British, French, Polish or Dominion troops but 'the position might have been different if there had been a United Ireland'.

The Chamberlain scenario was proving uncannily precise and MacDonald took his cue and suggested that a step might be taken towards the project of a united Ireland by the establishment of a joint council for the defence of the whole island. 'This, however, Mr de Valera had rejected as a step involving a decisive breach of neutrality and as a blow to the national unity of Eire.' MacDonald's brief did not permit him to go any further along the primrose path to the united Ireland so he changed the subject and appealed to de Valera 'to improve the immediate prospect by arresting and imprisoning the IRA leaders and interning suspect Germans and Italians'. MacDonald was on weak ground here as ten days earlier 390 IRA suspects had been arrested and interned. There were about 300 German nationals in the country many of them women and children and in a report in May 1945 Maffey was to describe this group as 'mostly harmless'.[8]

If de Valera intended to impress MacDonald with his determination to hold to neutrality to the last possible moment he succeeded, because the latter told the war cabinet that de Valera 'was genuine in his determination to resist either belligerent to the utmost limit of his power; this resistance would be directed against any attempt on our part to seize the Atlantic ports by force'.

Chamberlain, freed of the responsibility of decision-making and already dying of cancer, had become a 'hawk' on the Irish neutrality question. He thanked MacDonald for 'instilling some sense of reality into Mr de Valera' although he had repeated the old theme that he could do nothing to prejudice his country's neutrality on which his much vaunted 'national unity' depended. Chamberlain had seen a preliminary draft of an *aide-mémoire* from the Chiefs of Staff which said that there could be 'no security for Eire or the United Kingdom' unless British or Dominion troops and ships were in Eire. It was further pointed out that the main and perhaps sole obstacle to such collaboration was the partition question.

Chamberlain went on to say that on the basis that help to Eire after invasion had taken place might well come too late, 'we were compelled to consider the question of entering the Irish ports by force'. But before this step was taken he would advocate further exploration of the ground in view especially of the possibly unfavourable reaction which would be caused in the USA by any forcible measures against Ireland. He would therefore propose that the Minister of Health would return to Dublin and tell Mr de Valera that there was no possibility of making his country safe against German invasion – of which it stood in imminent danger – unless he gave the British navy the use of the Atlantic ports, allowed their troops and air forces to enter the country before the invasion, and interned all IRA leaders still at large and suspicious Germans and Italians.

The *quid pro quo* would be 'a declaration stating that His Majesty's Government were, in principle, in favour of the establishment of a United Ireland'. Chamberlain went on:

> This would naturally have to be followed by an approach to Lord Craigavon, who would have to be told that the interests of Northern Ireland could not be allowed to stand against the vital interests of the British Empire. Lord Craigavon would naturally ask whether the United Ireland would form part of the British Empire. The answer to this was clearly in the affirmative, though of course full Dominion status carried with it the right to secede from the Commonwealth. Should Mr de Valera still maintain a negative attitude, the Minister of Health should insist that the proposition should be put to his Government, some members of which he [Chamberlain] understood were likely to take a less rigid view.

If the Irish government's refusal was still maintained, Chamberlain added, the British government would be on stronger ground *vis à vis* the United States if later on they were compelled to use force.

Churchill came in at this stage of the discussion to say that while agreeing generally with Chamberlain, they must avoid putting undue pressure on 'the loyal province of Ulster'. He would not urge those who had worked self-government loyally within the Empire to join with those who wished to stay outside it. He was not convinced that the military situation was as serious as it had been represented. He was in favour of allowing the enemy to make the first move; if they succeeded in establishing themselves in Ireland their forces should then be ready to pounce upon them. The whole of Ireland, including Mr de Valera, would in those circumstances be on their side.

One cannot help comparing the situation with that of the previous October when Churchill was arguing strongly for the forcible take-over of the Irish ports and Chamberlain was the one to point out the dangers. Another irony was in the fact that the Orangemen who threatened to kill Churchill when he went to Belfast in 1912 as a Liberal Home Rule champion, would have cheered him to the echo if they could have heard him standing up for them now.

Chamberlain seemed embarrassed as one by one his cabinet colleagues took a more flexible view and the proposal of the Foreign Secretary, Lord Halifax, was adopted. This was that Mr MacDonald should return to Dublin 'where he could continue the process of educating Mr de Valera as to the dangers of invasion, at the same time exploring to what extent any advance towards a United Ireland would help Mr de Valera in dealing with Irish opinion on this matter. If anything useful came out of these conversations, it would, of course, have to be put to Lord Craigavon.'

Malcolm MacDonald accordingly went back to Dublin and he asked Mr de Valera whether there were any circumstances under which the Irish government would be prepared, before a German invasion started, to invite British ships, troops and planes into its territory and to take action against the fifth column. The discussion that followed centred around three possibilities:[9]

> 1 That there should be a declaration of a United Ireland in principle, the constitutional and other practical details of the Union to be worked out in due course; Ulster to remain a belligerent, Eire to remain neutral, at any rate for the time being; if both parties desired it, a joint Defence Council to be set up at once; at the same time, British naval ships to be allowed into Eire ports, British troops and aeroplanes to be stationed at certain agreed points in the territory, the British Government to provide additional equipment for Eire's forces, and the Eire Government to take effective action against the Fifth Column.

Mr de Valera emphatically rejected this suggestion saying the admission of British forces would be regarded as an abandonment of neutrality and would break the 'national unity'. Besides there was a grave danger of the British troops being fired on by extremists. His government would hold this view as well as himself. Mr de Valera then made his own proposal which was the second of these possibilities:

> 2 That Eire and Ulster should be merged in a United Ireland which would at once become neutral; its neutrality to be guaranteed by Great Britain and the United States of America; since Britain was a belligerent its military and naval forces should not take any active part in guaranteeing that neutrality, but American ships could come into the Irish ports, and perhaps American troops into Ireland, to effect this guarantee.

But MacDonald, in his turn, rejected this proposal 'for a number of reasons which are obvious' as he said in his report to the war cabinet. The third possibility was a compromise:

> 3 That there should be a declaration of a United Ireland in principle, the constitutional and practical details of the Union to be worked out in due

Page 51
Mr Malcolm MacDonald,
Minister of Health in the
British government, who
came to Dublin three times
in June 1940 in an unavailing
attempt to persuade Mr de
Valera to enter the war in
exchange for a scheme for
Irish unity.

The Irish infantryman of
September 1939 wore a
German-style helmet, tunic
and breeches of very dark
green wool mixture and stiff
leather leggings. In 1940 a
British-style helmet and
uniform were adopted with a
lighter grey-green colour.

Page 52 (above) *In London in April 1940 for Anglo-Irish trade talks which proved unsuccessful were, from left: Mr John Leydon (Secretary, Department of Supplies); Mr Sean Lemass (Minister for Supplies); Mr John Dulanty (Irish High Commissioner); Dr James Ryan (Minister for Agriculture). The Lemass-Leydon team later showed outstanding ingenuity in keeping Ireland supplied with vital foodstuffs and essential materials for home industries; (below) the aftermath of the German air-raid on the North Strand area of Dublin in May 1941. The toll was: 27 killed, 45 hurt, 25 houses destroyed and 300 damaged. The German government paid compensation over twenty years later.*

course; this United Ireland to become at once a belligerent on the side of the Allies.

On this, Mr de Valera said that if there was not only a declaration of a united Ireland in principle, but also agreement upon its constitution, then the government of Eire *might* (MacDonald's italics) agree to enter the war at once. He could not be certain about this. Perhaps the existing government would not agree to it and would be replaced by another government which did.

Mr MacDonald replied that, quite apart from other difficulties, he saw two practical objections to Mr de Valera's suggestion. First, he saw no chance of a constitution being prepared and agreed to in the short time which might be at their disposal before invasion took place, and secondly, the government in London could not be satisfied with a vague assurance that the Eire government 'might' enter the war, since again the issue was urgent, and they could not approach the Ulster authorities with any proposal of the kind suggested unless they had a firm assurance that the government of Eire would, in fact, come into the war.

Mr de Valera replied that he could not go further than 'might' with a big question-mark after that 'might'. When Mr MacDonald asked whether he could report that this was the view not only of Mr de Valera himself, but also of the other members of his government, Mr de Valera after some hesitation said that he would cast his own vote that way, but that perhaps some of his colleagues would take a different view. But he did not think they would. His chief reason for this attitude was that his people were really almost completely unprepared for war. They had not a well-equipped army, nor had they guns to resist tanks and mechanised troops. Dublin was practically an undefended city, where there were only a few anti-aircraft guns and no air-raid shelters or gas masks for the citizens. The people would be mercilessly exposed to the horrors of modern war, and he could not have borne it on his conscience that in this state of affairs he had taken the initiative in an action which led to war. If the initiative were taken by German invaders, that was another matter. He and his people would resist bitterly.

Whether he realised it or not Mr de Valera had now been manoeuvred into the position where the question of military equipment was be-

D

coming a key factor, and not surprisingly MacDonald pressed hard on this point. Once the Irish government had agreed to enter the war on the British side, he said, that would alter their attitude on the question of equipment for Irish forces and with British ships in Irish ports and British troops side by side with Irish ones to defend strategic points that assurance 'would enable us to send such guns, rifles and ammunition, and such gas masks and other equipment for passive defence' as could be spared. Sensing, perhaps, the advantage he had given MacDonald in the discussion, de Valera would not be drawn further and said he would report the discussion to his cabinet colleagues.

Chamberlain told the war cabinet that Sir John Maffey's view was that the Irish cabinet would have been ready to agree to such a proposal two or three months ago, but that their views had been somewhat influenced by the recent German successes (France had capitulated the day before). Nevertheless Maffey thought that some of the Irish ministers might be prepared to support a declaration of war on these conditions now, and Chamberlain proposed to test this by holding out the bait of military equipment. His plan was that Mr de Valera should be asked definitely what would be the attitude of his government to the following plan, to which, if it were accepted, the government in London would do their best to obtain the assent of the Ulster government. (*a*) A declaration of a united Ireland in principle; (*b*) a joint body including representatives of the government of Eire and Northern Ireland to be set up at once to work out the constitutional and other practical details of the union. The government in London to give such assistance as might be desired; (*c*) a joint Defence Council to be set up immediately; (*d*) Eire to join the war on the British side forthwith and for the purposes of the defence of Eire, permission to be given for British naval vessels to have the use of Southern Irish ports and for British troops and aeroplanes to be stationed in such positions in Eire as may be agreed with the Eire government; (*e*) the Eire government to intern all enemy aliens in the country and to take any steps necessary to suppress fifth column activities; (*f*) the British government to provide equipment as early as possible to the Eire government in accordance with the particulars given in the appendix to the plan.

Chamberlain suggested that if the war cabinet agreed to this plan, MacDonald should take it to Dublin himself and wait for the reply of the Eire government. If that reply was favourable he did not believe the Ulster government would refuse to play their part in bringing about so favourable a development. But he believed the answer from Dublin would probably be negative and all they could do then was take further efforts to improve relations. The war cabinet agreed to MacDonald bringing over the new plan, and invited Chamberlain to write to Lord Craigavon informally, indicating to him in broad outline the nature of the communication being made to Mr de Valera.

For the third time in ten days MacDonald flew to Dublin and he presented de Valera with a memorandum of the six-point plan which was practically word for word with that set out by Chamberlain. The following day, 27 June, MacDonald telegraphed his report back to London. It is worth quoting at some length:

> Mr de Valera discussed plan with his colleagues this morning and I had conversation with him, Lemass and Aiken this afternoon. This was most unsatisfactory. Aiken who did most of the talking on their side was even more persistent than de Valera himself has been in urging that the proper solution is United Ireland which is neutral. I again stated that this is entirely out of the question, and repeated reasons for this. Lemass seemed to be prepared to discuss our plan in a more reasonable way, but his contributions to discussion were usually cut short by fresh uncompromising interventions from one or other of his colleagues. I got the impression that de Valera had not passed on to his colleagues the assurance I gave him yesterday that declaration of a United Ireland should settle the issue once and for all, and that there would be no going back on that, for he said that one of the principal reasons why his Cabinet regard the plan as unacceptable is that they believe that United Ireland will not materialise from it. I repeated my assurances to all three Ministers and told them that if they rejected the plan on this ground it was a false point. I think Lemass, and even Aiken, was impressed. I think it would strengthen our position if we amended the document by insertion of words which would give specific assurance on this point. Lemass, but not others, also seemed a bit influenced when I said that we would be sufficiently content if Eire did not positively enter the war, but remained neutral and invited our ships into her ports and our troops and aeroplanes into her territory as additional defence against violation of that neutrality. I am definitely of opinion that the Cabinet here will reject our plan. But in my opinion it would be wise to make amendment suggested above and also certain other amendments in the document so as to bring out more clearly the specific advantages to people of Eire inherent in plan, and avoid possibility of Eire Government rejecting it on grounds which misrepresent its real substance.

The weakness in MacDonald's negotiating position so far was, of course, his inability to speak for Craigavon, and de Valera had only too vivid memories of how Craigavon as Sir James Craig had stubbornly fended off all efforts by the 'Welsh wizard' himself, Lloyd George, in the 1921 negotiations to compromise Northern Ireland's position within the United Kingdom. Consequently, it is difficult to see how MacDonald could have been so sure that 'declaration of a United Ireland should settle the issue once and for all'. When the war cabinet met on 28 June to discuss MacDonald's report, Chamberlain is recorded as saying that

> he had written to Lord Craigavon indicating to him the nature of the plan outlined in the Memorandum which had been handed to Mr de Valera. The reply received had been to the effect that Lord Craigavon was shocked to learn that negotiations were being carried on behind Ulster's back. Such an accusation was, of course, entirely unjustified. All that the Government had done was to enquire what would be the attitude of the Government of Eire towards a certain plan. It had throughout been made clear that it would be necessary to obtain the assent thereto of the Government of Northern Ireland.

This salvo from Craigavon, even in the restrained language of the cabinet minutes, had the desired effect and it was agreed that a reply should be sent to him 'emphasising that Northern Ireland's position was entirely protected'. The cabinet then went on to discuss in rather disillusioned fashion the changes in the plan which MacDonald advocated. MacDonald said he thought there was a minority in Mr de Valera's cabinet who would be ready for discussions on the basis of the plan outlined. The modifications now proposed in the plan would be helpful to this minority but he feared it was unlikely to affect the majority view.

The following morning, 29 June, de Valera was handed the letter from Chamberlain incorporating the proposed changes in the plan. The letter said drily:

> I would remind you that the whole plan depends upon our obtaining the assent of Northern Ireland, and it seems to me that if this is done there can be no reason to doubt that the plan will be carried out in its entirety. I cannot, of course, give a guarantee that Northern Ireland will assent [recalling Craigavon's 'shock', Chamberlain's tongue must have been well in cheek] but if the plan is accepted by Eire we should do our best to persuade Northern Ireland to accept it also in the interests of the security of the whole island.

The amendments are interesting as an indication of how far the British position had moved towards unity since the first approach with its meagre all-Ireland Council of Defence. The first and second subparagraphs were now to read:

(i) A declaration to be made by the United Kingdom Government forthwith accepting the principle of a United Ireland. This declaration would take the form of a solemn undertaking that the Union is to become at an early date an accomplished fact from which there shall be no turning back.
(ii) A joint Body including representatives of the Government of Eire and the Government of Northern Ireland, to be set up at once to work out the constitutional and other practical details of the Union of Ireland. The United Kingdom Government to give such assistance towards the work of this Body as might be desired, the purpose of the work being to establish at as early a date as possible the whole machinery of Government of the Union.

Chamberlain went on to say that he understood that de Valera had suggested that it would be desirable that the parliaments of Eire and of Ulster should meet together immediately, with sovereign powers to legislate for the whole of Ireland on matters of common concern, pending the working out and more permanent establishment of the constitution of the union. De Valera had suggested this to MacDonald because he did not think that the setting up of a Joint Defence Council by itself in the first instance would be sufficient to demonstrate to the people in the south the 'genuineness of the change towards the Union of Ireland'. Chamberlain said such a formal suggestion would be given immediate consideration 'with every desire to reach an arrangement satisfactory to all the parties concerned'.

It is interesting to speculate, especially in view of the crisis in Northern Ireland since 1969, how seriously de Valera considered the prospect of abandoning neutrality in exchange for unity. A few weeks later de Valera told Maffey that 'it had gone hard with him to turn down any scheme which would bring about a united Ireland, the dream of his life. But in the present circumstances acceptance would have been impossible. It would have meant civil war.' 'His regret was genuine,' wrote Maffey, 'and he asked me to mention this to Mr Neville Chamberlain and to let him know how he felt about it.'[10] The tragic example of John Redmond in 1914 must have weighed heavily with de Valera and his cabinet who would all remember only too vividly how the famous

Irish Parliamentary Party leader sent tens of thousands of young Irish-men to fight for little Belgium having been promised Home Rule for all Ireland when the war was over.

Given de Valera's immense prestige and dominant personality it is unlikely that there was any chance of a serious split in the cabinet over the British plan as MacDonald had optimistically hoped. But in his letter of 4 July to Chamberlain rejecting the plan, de Valera seemed on the defensive: 'The plan would commit us definitely to an immediate abandonment of our neutrality. On the other hand, it gives no guaran-tee that in the end we would have a United Ireland unless indeed concessions were made to Lord Craigavon opposed to the sentiments and aspirations of the great majority of the Irish people.'

If Ireland with a copper-fastened guarantee of unity were fighting on the side of Britain when she was standing alone in Europe against Hitler, one wonders what were the concessions to Craigavon which de Valera so greatly feared. He had deliberately kept nominal, if ambigu-ous, Dominion status for the south in his 1937 constitution to facilitate future accommodation with the north in any unity moves, and Craigavon could scarcely have demanded the reintegration of the whole country back into the United Kingdom. What has not been revealed is how seriously the war cabinet tried to obtain Craigavon's assent to the unity plan. The evidence suggests that it made no attempt at all.

We have seen Churchill's objection to any coercion of the Ulster loyalists and the cabinet's hasty reaction to Craigavon's letter of 'shock'. On 30 June, while de Valera was still studying the latest amendments to the unity plan, Craigavon addressed an Orange meeting at Kirkis-town, Co Down, and referred to recent speeches suggesting Ulster should agree to a united Ireland.

Craigavon said that de Valera was again blackmailing the British government to end partition. He would not be a party to any change in the constitutional status. Nevertheless he was prepared to enter into the closest co-operation with de Valera on defence 'provided he takes a stand, as we are doing, on the side of Britain and the Empire, cleared out the German and Italian representatives from the twenty-six counties and undertook not to raise any issue of a constitutional nature'.

Here was the authentic voice of loyalist Ulster, and de Valera was surely right when he said that the unity plan was a recipe for civil war as it stood. A prominent Irish senator, Frank MacDermot, unaware of these secret negotiations, travelled north about this time to have a talk with a northern minister, Mr Basil Brooke, later to become prime minister, and Lord Brookeborough. He was certainly one of the hard-line men on keeping Ulster British but in those grim days after Dunkirk he told the southern senator that if Eire gave the ports to Britain in return for unity after the war, it would cause a split in the northern cabinet but he personally would have felt obliged to vote in favour of it. Another interesting little curio for the museum of 'what might have been'.

Notes to this chapter are on p 180

Chapter 4

Germany Tries Her Hand

———◆———

The recruiting drive launched in Ireland in the last days of May 1940, and the setting up of a defence conference grouping government ministers and leaders of the opposition parties, was observed with special interest in Germany. Reporting the Irish warlike preparations, Berlin Radio commented: 'It is to be hoped that everything will be done to preserve the neutrality of that country. It will at any rate be a precedent as there has never been a war yet but the Irish were fighting.'[1]

The German minister in Dublin, Dr Hempel, could not permit himself such touches of humour as he tried to assess the effect on Irish opinion of the German successes in Holland, Belgium and France. He reported that feeling towards Germany had 'noticeably deteriorated' especially among church circles who had been strongly influenced by the recent attitude of the Pope. Even among Irish nationalists the German successes seemed to have no real impact. In any case, de Valera, 'still the only recognised political leader of larger stature', had the nationalist elements well in hand and Hempel shrewdly predicted: 'He will maintain friendly understanding with England as far as possible on account of the geographical and economic dependence which will continue even if England is defeated, as well as his democratic principles, even in face of the threatening danger of Ireland becoming involved in the war.'[2]

From the time of the IRA's 'declaration of war' on Britain in January 1939 there was always the danger that Hempel's professional diplomacy would be undermined by a clumsy intervention in Irish affairs by the Abwehr, the German military secret service headed by the ill-fated Admiral Canaris. Abwehr II under Colonel Lahousen specialised in sabotage operations against the enemy and so was especially interested in the potential offered by IRA saboteurs for operations in Northern Ireland and to a lesser extent in Britain. Hempel had no sooner sent off the report mentioned above than the blow fell – the Irish police raiding Stephen Carroll Held's house in Dublin on the night of 22 May found unmistakable traces in a locked room of the recent sojourn of a German parachutist and, even more alarming, a crude plan for a German sea landing near Derry in Northern Ireland to be supported by an IRA force crossing the border from Co Leitrim. Known as Plan Kathleen and also the Artus Plan, it had been brought to Germany the previous month by Held himself who was used by the IRA as a link with Germany because of his German father. The plan was so ludicrous that it had been rejected out of hand by the Abwehr, but the Irish security authorities could not be expected to know this.

Held told the police that the incriminating documents, parachute, wireless set and $20,000 belonged to a mysterious visitor called Brandy who had since vanished. He had, in fact, hopped over a wall at the first sight of the police car, and for this stupid mistake the police had to wait another eighteen months before finally arresting him. Brandy was none other than Captain Hermann Goertz, Luftwaffe officer, doctor of law and a secret agent for Abwehr II who had parachuted him into Ireland a few weeks earlier for the mission of using the IRA for sabotage operations in Northern Ireland and making contact with Irish people of pro-German sympathies. The full story of Goertz and the other dozen German agents sent to Ireland during the war is told in Enno Stephan's well-researched *Spies in Ireland*. Due to sloppy planning and the Abwehr's poor intelligence about conditions in Ireland, with the exception of Goertz they were all picked up within days or even hours of landing. Hempel's reporting was probably of more value to Germany than all the Abwehr's misguided espionage operations which a former Abwehr officer, Paul Leverkuehn, describes as 'quite insignificant and without any military effect on the course of the war'.[3]

With hindsight this is now quite obvious, but on 24 May 1940 the Irish authorities were in a state of shock and Hempel was dashing off a 'Most Urgent, Top Secret' telegram to Berlin (via the German embassy in Washington which radioed it to the Foreign Ministry) report-

ing the arrest of Held and the opening of his case before the Special
Criminal Court. The next day there was a further alarming develop-
ment for Hempel to report when Mrs Iseult Stuart was remanded by
the court on similar charges to Held. She was a daughter of the famous
Maud Gonne MacBride and a sister of Sean MacBride, a former IRA
Chief of Staff, a brilliant advocate and a future foreign minister. Her
involvement with Goertz, alias Brandy, was through her husband, the
writer Francis Stuart, who was then teaching in Berlin and had given
Goertz his address in Laragh, Co Wicklow, as a possible refuge.
Goertz hid there for some days after his parachute landing, and Mrs
Stuart bought clothes for him in Dublin which were found in Held's
house and easily traced.

What especially perturbed Hempel and his superiors in Berlin was
the Irish government's apparent determination to give the affair full
publicity by allowing the newspapers to report the court proceedings.
Hempel commented sadly: 'The affair has thereby turned unmistakably
against us and upsets all pretexts of English intrigues.' He feared that
the publicity would cause a 'critical undermining' of the German
position in Ireland. He would have been even more depressed if he had
known that at that very time Lt-Colonel Dudley Clarke was having
secret liaison talks with the Irish army staff in Dublin in anticipation of
a German invasion. It was little consolation when Berlin informed
Hempel that Goertz's mission was directed 'exclusively against
England' and that any activity against the Irish government was
'expressly forbidden'.

The Goertz affair had the effect, however, of making Berlin think
out the exact nature of their Irish policy as, contrary to what Chamberlain and the war cabinet believed, it was certainly not an invasion. On
15 June, when Malcolm MacDonald was getting ready for his first
visit to Dublin, Woermann sent Hempel the following statement
which he was ordered to make to the Irish government concerning the
Held-Stuart case:

> We considered it important to inform the Irish Government once again
> that our sole object in the struggle was England. We believed that Ireland,
> whose enemy through history was known to be England, was fully aware
> that the outcome of this struggle would also be of decisive importance for
> the Irish nation and the *final realisation of its national demands* [author's
> italics]. Given this situation we believed that we could also count on the

greatest possible understanding from the Irish Government, despite its neutral attitude, even if Ireland might in some ways be affected by our measures.

This carefully phrased statement was to be followed by a warning that matters such as the charges against Held should also be treated in a correspondingly careful manner by the Irish government and above all in the Press. Two days later, Hempel went along to see Walshe in the Department of External Affairs and he was gratified to find Walshe expressing 'great admiration for German achievements'. These presumably included the invasion of the Low Countries against which de Valera had protested the month before. The protest season had quickly closed and Walshe seems to have become convinced that Germany would soon win the war, an impression confirmed to the author by an Irish parliamentarian who had a long talk with Walshe around this time. There was nothing especially remarkable about such a view in June 1940 and it was also held by the US ambassador to Britain, Mr Joseph Kennedy, the aviator Charles Lindbergh, and Benito Mussolini to mention only a few. This did not mean that Walshe was pro-Nazi. As a highly educated and well-informed man who had once studied for the priesthood and whose ambition was to be ambassador to the Vatican, he must have felt a deep revulsion for the Nazi persecution of the Catholic Church in Germany and Poland of which Walshe was certainly aware but which censorship carefully kept from the Irish public.

When Hempel got around to reading the instructions quoted above, Walshe misinterpreted them and assumed that he was being told indirectly that the Germans were going to be forced to invade Ireland to achieve the conquest of Britain.[4] It took some time before Hempel could remove this misunderstanding, but Walshe eventually got the message about the Held case and he then relaxed, confiding that England was Ireland's main fear. He referred to a recent interview Hitler gave to a Hearst newspaper reaffirming his intention not to destroy the British Empire, saying he hoped this did not mean 'the abandonment of Ireland' and showing special interest in the cryptic phrase the 'final realisation' of Irish national demands. Hempel guessed rightly that this would mean a further talk with de Valera himself.

On 18 June, the day after MacDonald had made his first tentative offer of a declaration of unity in exchange for the abandonment of

Irish neutrality, de Valera received Hempel with Walshe present. The latter 'readily supported' Hempel's request for no further publicity for the Held case, while de Valera was at pains to impress Hempel with Ireland's continued adherence to strict neutrality which, in spite of Irish fears, Britain had so far respected. With regard to the solution of the Northern Ireland question, de Valera told Hempel that 'he must, in view of the English-Irish power relationship, adhere to a peaceful solution, as only so could a permanent and tenable position be reached'.

Hempel was remarkably well informed of what was afoot concerning the Anglo-Irish unity move and he even knew that the new American minister to Ireland, David Gray, had been playing a part. Gray in fact had travelled to Belfast with Maffey urging him to sound out Craigavon on the unity plan but found him 'quite unmoved by any instructions he may have had from London. Craigavon was in no compromising mood and flatly declined to take any initiative to end the dispute with Eire.'[5]

Hempel was anxious lest de Valera should crack under the British pressure, especially as Irish fears of a German invasion did not seem to have diminished following the Held case. Hempel reported to Berlin on 1 July that he was convinced that the Irish government, in spite of the difficulties, wanted to do everything possible to maintain neutrality and that 'particularly Walshe and Boland are exercising a strong influence on de Valera in this direction'. In a meeting with the Italian minister, Vincenzo Berardis, de Valera, according to Hempel, had tried 'particularly to elicit a reassuring statement from the Axis powers that there was no intention of an attack on Ireland.

The Reich Foreign Minister, Ribbentrop, now intervened personally to instruct Hempel on 11 July to emphasise in all conversations that in connection with Ireland, Germany's exclusive interest was the maintenance of her neutrality. He continued:

> Accordingly it is an utterly unreasonable suspicion that we might have the intention to prepare to use Ireland as a military base against England through a so-called 'fifth column' which besides does not exist. If the British Government in dealing with the Irish Government makes use of the idea of a union of Northern Ireland with Southern Ireland, it is evident that this is only a sham which is only engaged in for the purposes of manoeuvring Ireland out of her neutrality and drawing her into the war.

In fact Ribbentrop was wrong on both counts. The British offer was not a sham. It was genuine but ineffective. Secondly, suspicions that Germany might want to use the IRA were anything but unreasonable, and at the moment of Ribbentrop's feigned indignation the Foreign Ministry with his express approval were co-operating with Abwehr II, in Operation Dove, to send back to Ireland the IRA leader Sean Russell who was being trained in Berlin in sabotage techniques although he knew a good few already himself. Russell had been in the USA raising money for the IRA campaign against Britain when the war broke out, and in January 1940 the Abwehr and the German Foreign Ministry began plotting to get him to Germany from where he could be brought to Ireland by submarine. Hempel advised against it but Ribbentrop took a personal interest and a memorandum by Woermann on 28 March laconically records Ribbentrop's decisions 'on the question of an Irish rebellion'. These were to assign the Foreign Ministry's *coup d'état* specialist, Dr Edmund Veesenmayer, to the Russell mission and to organise his escape from the USA where he was being closely shadowed by American and British intelligence agents.

The Foreign Ministry and the Abwehr also entered into close liaison to arrange for the release of another well-known IRA leader, Frank Ryan, from prison in Spain, where he had fought in the Civil War on the republican side, had been captured, sentenced to death and reprieved after a personal plea to Franco by Ryan's old republican comrade, de Valera. Ryan was also brought to Berlin and although in poor health it was planned to send him back to Ireland with Russell by submarine. Russell and Ryan had been bitter opponents within the IRA. To use modern parlance Russell represented the 'Provisional' tendency – the traditional amalgam of fervent Catholicism (he went to Mass regularly in Berlin) and hatred of Britain. Ryan belonged to the 'Official' tendency – the breakaway left-wing faction which saw Irish freedom as incomplete without a socialist revolution.

Russell was to be given a free hand in Ireland after his return to take whatever action he thought appropriate, and if joint activities with the Germans became possible the signal for the IRA would be a red flowerpot on a special window-sill of the German legation in Dublin. But Operation Dove ended in tragedy. A week after the submarine with the two Irishmen left Germany, Sean Russell died on board on 15 August almost within sight of Ireland. Ryan, who had not apparently been fully briefed on Russell's mission, decided to return to Germany where his health worsened and he died there in June 1944.

During July, Hempel was continuing to find Walshe in External Affairs anticipating a British defeat or some attempt to sue for peace and he wanted to ensure Irish interests would be looked after. Hempel reported on 31 July:

> From various indications in talks with Walshe and Boland I assume that the Irish Government may be placing hope in future German interest in the maintenance and completion of an entirely independent United Irish State. They express this in a rather negative fashion by saying that they hope that in a future peace settlement we will not sacrifice Ireland to England, or they speak of negotiations which the Irish Government will have to carry on with us then.[6]

Hempel added that the special fear was that England would try and compensate for the loss of the Empire by reducing Ireland to the old position of dependence.

De Valera was, however, conducting a subtle diplomatic game, letting his subordinates have enigmatic conversations with Hempel about what might happen if Germany won the war while he endeavoured to bring Anglo-Irish relations on to a better footing. He asked Maffey to see him and on 17 July they had a long talk which was reported to the war cabinet. De Valera told Maffey he wanted to discuss the deterioration in the relationship between the two countries and to find ways and means of getting back to the *status quo ante*.[7]

He went on to list the causes for the deterioration as first, the serious stage reached in the war which could lead Britain to seek 'at all costs' the use of air bases and ports in Eire. Secondly, there was the Press campaign criticising Eire for her neutrality and it was of such proportions that it suggested permission or connivance. America had come in on the same note and in Ireland all this had been taken as British propaganda implying stronger measures to follow. In America important sections of the Irish community who had always been unfriendly to de Valera personally had smelt a danger and had rallied to his support. This was significant. There were other more subtle causes, de Valera went on, all combining to give the impression that the British were almost eager for the Germans to come in so that they could get in themselves. Talk of a military pact had been published and had done great harm. He begged that their military and staff liaison should be kept as secret as possible.

De Valera then referred to the case of Major Byass, the British officer from the north, who had been engaged in some form of espionage in Eire. Maffey's report continued:

> The staff work of his Army in recent years had been directed at meeting an attack from us. With the outbreak of war they had switched over completely to plans for defeating aggression by Germany. He was bound to tell me that he had recently told the General Staff by no means to exclude the earlier possibility. In fact, he was not exaggerating when he told me that the expectation of invasion by us was now far more general than expectation of any other alternative. The Byass affair was a source of much perturbation among his Army officers. They said: 'We have shown these people everything. We have revealed our plans. But there is something more they want. What are we to think?'

Maffey had cleverly anticipated just such an embarrassing moment and he produced a telegram from the War Office saying that Byass had been on leave but had been instructed to collect information of military interest about roads etc in Eire but this had been done without the consent of the War Office, and the GOC in the north had been told not to let such a thing occur again without prior consultation with the Eire authorities. The telegram went on to say that in view of the fact that Byass's action was taken 'in a genuine attempt to prepare ourselves for giving assistance to the Eire Government if they invited us to do so in the case of an emergency' the War Office hoped their apology would be accepted and Byass released forthwith. They also hoped nothing would appear in the Press about it.

Maffey reported that the telegram had 'a tremendous effect' and he felt the whole atmosphere change. The officer was to be released at once. The conversation then switched to Eire's need for arms and equipment and de Valera said that the British failure to help had also lent colour to the idea that they wanted to come in and do the job themselves. Maffey protested that the real difficulty was Britain's own desperate need and in masterly fashion produced from his pocket another telegram, this time from the British ambassador in Washington indicating that they were giving all the help they could through the British Purchasing Commission in the USA to get Eire's request for arms and equipment there fulfilled. The previous June de Valera had

appealed directly to Washington for armoured cars, fighters and rifles
and Roosevelt had passed the buck to the British Purchasing Commission.

Maffey's two telegrams clearly won de Valera over from his previous
mistrust and his usual reserve dropped momentarily. He begged
Maffey earnestly to do his best in London to get him 'a few' anti-tank
guns, fighters and anti-aircraft guns as Dublin must be defended.
'Everything would go if the Government deserted it. It could not
possibly be declared an open town,' he said, and went on:

> Why will you not trust us? If you think we might attack the North I say
> with all emphasis we will never do that. No solution there can come by
> force. There we must now wait and let the solution come with time and
> patience. If you think the IRA will get the arms, I can assure you that we
> have no fifth column today. There is no danger in that quarter.
>   Give us help with arms and we will fight the Germans as only Irishmen
> in their own country can fight. There is no doubt on which side my
> sympathies lie. Nowadays some people joke about my becoming pro-
> British. The cause I am urging on you is in the best interest of my own
> country and that is what matters most to me.

Lord Caldecote, the Dominions Secretary, was obviously impressed
by Maffey's report and he proposed to the war cabinet that three steps
should be taken to improve relations between Dublin and London. The
first would be to damp down the Press campaign which de Valera had
complained about: 'the Press have had a good run for some weeks, and
I hope they will respond to this hint'. The second step would be a
declaration by the prime minister in the House of Commons that
Britain had no intention of sending their forces into Eire without a
request from the government of Eire. The third step would be to release some of the arms and equipment which were to be given to Eire
under the MacDonald plan as this 'would go a long way towards
making Eire a friendly non-belligerent who would in case of invasion
develop into an active ally'. It is quite clear, incidentally, from Caldecote's memorandum that there was no British intention, certainly at
this stage, to invade Ireland either to seize the ports or to pre-empt a
German invasion. A very senior officer in the Irish army at that time
told the author that their intelligence service, through an Irishman in
the British forces, succeeded in getting a copy of a British contingency
plan to invade Eire from the north with columns advancing down the

east coast, the east midlands and along the Shannon, the main objective being to overrun the Curragh military camp and then wheel left to take Dublin. Irish intelligence also got its hands on a British black-list of prominent Irish people whom they would arrest in such circumstances, and prominent on it was Walshe of External Affairs.

It is not surprising that an 'invasion plan' should have been drawn up by the British for use in certain contingencies and in fact it is remarkably like the W plan, which will be referred to later, to be activated when the Irish government asked for British help in the event of a German invasion. Nevertheless, all the evidence available now suggests that a British invasion of Ireland was never really contemplated.

Caldecote's proposals on improving relations with Dublin were studied by the war cabinet on 22 July, but objections were made to the non-invasion declaration and the supply of military equipment. Four days later the cabinet did authorise a supply of equipment which included anti-aircraft guns, ammunition, Bren carriers, searchlights and steel helmets. The helmets, the minutes recorded, would have a 'useful psychological effect' – perhaps a reference to the Irish army's use until recently of the German style coal-scuttle helmets.

As the month of September 1940 passed, the German threat to invade Britain also faded with the Luftwaffe's failure to smash the RAF in the Battle of Britain. The German invasion plan code-named Sea Lion intended the main landings to be on the south and south-east coast of England followed by a quick, powerful thrust for London; but to lessen the resistance in the landing areas several feint operations were also planned against the east coast from Norway and Holland code-named Autumn Journey. A third feint called Operation Green was to be a simulated landing in southern Ireland by five or six German divisions based on the French Atlantic coast. The feint operations were to look as realistic as possible with arrangements for the assembly and transfer of troops to be made and invasion training carried out. Admiral Canaris, head of the Abwehr, was instructed to ensure that this intelligence filtered through to the British authorities by various clandestine means.[8] This could be the explanation for Maffey telling de Valera on 14 July that British intelligence had learned that the invasion of Ireland was to take place the next day!

The government had some contingency plans ready if an invasion had taken place. An Emergency Powers Order allowed for the replace-

E

ment of the Taoiseach or other ministers if it became necessary. Regional and country commissioners on the British model were appointed whose main task would be to administer the public services in the event of an enemy attack isolating part of the country. A nation-wide link-up of parish councils would help to cope with the difficult supply situation which would then arise. There was heady talk in newspapers and elsewhere of how local patriotism could delay an invader and how the army would be able to adapt quickly to the traditional guerrilla-style warfare which had proved itself against the British in 1919–21. Mr Erskine Childers now President of Ireland but then a young deputy on the government benches urged: 'Each cottage, each village, each town must be a fortress in itself. If we were attacked, twenty armed men in some remote parish who could delay the passage of troops might well prove to be a turning point in our defence.'

Army headquarters was to be moved from Dublin, which would be extremely vulnerable to air attack in the event of invasion, to the de Vesci estate near Abbeyleix about fifty miles to the south-west. If the situation became completely hopeless, de Valera, senior ministers and some officials would be supplied with blue tickets which would get them a passage on a clipper to the USA from the seaplane base at Foynes. If possible the country's gold reserves would travel with the group to help in setting up a government in exile. It was about this time also that de Valera ordered the records of discussions with foreign diplomats in the Department of External Affairs to be destroyed as he feared that if they were captured by the Germans in the event of an invasion, they could be used for a *post facto* justification for the violation of neutrality as had happened in the case of Holland. This explains why there are scarcely any Irish official records of the diplomatic ex-changes of this and the later periods apart from some memoranda in de Valera's own personal papers. But Maffey's invaluable reports, for the accuracy of which de Valera himself has vouched in some cases, for-tunately fill the gap, as do Hempel's despatches.

No sooner had the threat of a German invasion of Britain and/or Ireland begun to recede than a fresh invasion scare blew up, this time that Britain was coming in to seize the ports. The British shipping losses on the Atlantic convoys, now routed around the north coast of Ireland following the fall of France, reached a record level in October 1940 and Churchill and his advisers wondered anxiously just how long

Britain could survive if the sinkings continued at this rate. His thoughts returned with renewed bitterness to the transfer of the Irish ports in 1938 and in a speech in the House of Commons on 6 November he complained that the fact that Britain could not use the south and west coasts of Ireland to refuel flotillas and aircraft which protected the trade by which Ireland as well as Britain lived, was 'a most heavy and grievous burden and one which should never have been placed upon our shoulders broad though they be'.

The speech itself did not cause real alarm in Dublin but it was the signal for a campaign to be unleashed in the British and even the American Press on the vital need of the Irish ports if Britain were to survive. An editorial in the usually level-headed *Economist* ran: 'If the ports become a matter of life and death – for Ireland as well as England – there can be only one way out: we must take them. That would of course revive all the old bitterness. But if bitterness there must be, let us have the bitterness *and* the bases, not the bitterness alone – which is all mere "retaliation" would provoke.'

This was bad enough but when George Bernard Shaw, probably Britain's best-known resident Irishman, also threw his rhetoric behind a British takeover of the ports, and on moral grounds to boot, de Valera was furious and denounced Shaw in an interview with Associated Press. What really stuck in Irish throats was Shaw's mocking tone:

> If I were in Churchill's place I should put it more philosophically. Instead of saying I will reoccupy your ports and leave you to do your damndest, I should say – 'My dear Mr de Valera, your policy is magnificent but it is not modern statesmanship. You say the ports belong to Ireland; that is what you start from. I cannot admit it. Local patriotism with all its heroic legends is as dead as a doornail today. The ports do not belong to Ireland: they belong to Europe, to the world, to civilisation, to the Most Holy Trinity, as you might say [a satirical reference to the Irish constitution], and are only held in trust by your Government in Dublin. In their names we must borrow the ports from you for the duration. You need not consent to the loan, just as you did not consent to the Treaty; and you will share all the advantages of our victory. All you have to do is to sit tight and say: "I protest!" England will do the rest. So here goes.'[9]

If it was any consolation to de Valera, at a later stage in the war Shaw admitted publicly that de Valera had done the right thing by sticking to neutrality and he admired his ability 'to get away with it'.

In the Dail de Valera, now almost blind, made an unusually im-

passioned speech in reply to Churchill saying there could be no
question of handing over the ports and any attempt to bring pressure
on them could only lead to bloodshed. He finished on a sombre note:
'I want to say to our people that we may be – I hope not – facing a
grave crisis. If we are to face it, then we shall do it, anyhow, knowing
that our cause is right and just and that if we have to die for it, we shall
be dying in that good cause.' Some people feel it was the finest speech
of his life, but the effect in the Dail was somewhat marred by the next
speaker, Deputy Hughes, resuming one of the innumerable and
tedious agricultural debates which preoccupied the Dail during these
years, with the words: 'I was speaking, Sir, of the grain situation.'[10]

Although Walshe told Hempel that Churchill's speech looked less
like a British intention to attack Ireland than an internal 'political
diversionary manoeuvre' because of the shipping losses, Hempel took
a more serious view and asked Berlin whether he should indicate to
de Valera, whom he had invited to lunch on 14 November, Germany's
willingness to help Ireland in the event of a British attack. That the
government were viewing the situation with less *sang-froid* than Walshe
was shown by Hempel also reporting that the Minister for Justice, Mr
Gerry Boland, on whom de Valera was leaning more and more, had
indicated that in the event of a British attack, a request for help to
Germany was 'actively under consideration'. Maffey at this time
reported de Valera in a 'very agitated and bitter mood' and Churchill
told the war cabinet that one line of approach would be to say that
Britain appreciated Eire's defenceless position and was prepared 'to go
to the limit of suffering before laying Eire open to German attacks but
if it became a matter of life and death, the United Kingdom might
have to take another view'.[11] Ironically enough it was just at this time
that arrangements were being finalised for Britain to take up Ireland's
offer to accept British refugees from German bombing.

Hempel's reports, coupled with the British and American Press campaign, had aroused great interest in Berlin and Weizacker, head of the
Foreign Ministry, advised that Hempel could say in the course of conversation with de Valera that Ireland's expected determined resistance
to a British attack 'would naturally lead to Ireland's being in a front
with us'. Weizacker continued: 'After England was finally crushed by
us, Ireland could then expect in an entirely altered situation to be able
to realise her national goals.' The inflexible Craigavon need not have

worried about such a prospect – a fortnight later he was dead with de Valera commenting: 'I am sorry. I liked him personally.'

The tense Anglo-Irish situation was now engaging the attention of no less a person than Hitler himself and a conversation between him and Ribbentrop on 26 November is briefly recorded. Ribbentrop said he was convinced the Irish would defend themselves to the utmost against England but that de Valera would not 'expose himself with respect to us' before an attack. He would ask Hempel to sound out de Valera on his intentions. The High Command was considering that if aid had to be given to Ireland, British war material captured at Dunkirk could be brought to Ireland from the French coast in Irish ships. Following his talk with Hitler, Ribbentrop sent Hempel an 'Immediate, Top Secret' message instructing him to sound out influential people, preferably de Valera himself, on whether German help would be sought in the case of a British attack. This was to be done in a roundabout fashion. Hempel could give most definite reassurances that Germany naturally had no intention of violating Irish neutrality, 'but if a British attack came, you could personally very well imagine that the Reich Government would be in a position to give Ireland vigorous support and would be inclined to do so'. Hempel was also to inquire discreetly by what ports and by which ships German aid could best be sent.

The Germans by now knew that there were strict limits on their ability to help Ireland in case of a British seizure of the ports. On 14 November Ambassador Ritter at the Foreign Ministry recorded a conversation with General Warlimont who had studied the Irish situation and concluded that the only help which could be given was: (*a*) concentration of German submarines around the Irish ports occupied by the British; (*b*) extension of Luftwaffe attacks to these ports. He saw no further possibilities. In particular, the commitment of air landing troops was out of the question since the absolutely necessary supplies could not be assured. So much for Chamberlain's panic estimates of the danger to Ireland from German paratroops the previous summer. By a strange coincidence he died the day Ritter wrote his memorandum and de Valera telegraphed his widow: 'Mr Chamberlain will always be remembered by the Irish people for his noble efforts in the cause of peace and friendship between the two nations.'

On 3 December, the Commander-in-Chief of the German navy, Admiral Raeder, presented Hitler with even more powerful arguments against attempting a sea landing in Ireland in the event of a British invasion.[12] The necessary naval supremacy was not there 'not even for the duration of one transport operation'. Second, the geographical position was extremely unfavourable with Wales and Cornwall extending like a wedge towards the German line of approach and vital supply line. Third, Ireland had no defended bases or anchorages at all and there would be no time for fortifying them or for an undisturbed disembarkation. Fourth, a defending force cut off in Ireland would have little protection from the topography from modern weapons as at Narvik, and sooner or later the German expeditionary force would meet a Dunkirk-like situation in face of the British expeditionary force brought over under protection of British naval power. Fifth, the air force would be hampered by heavy rainfall, low clouds and fog. Air support would have to come from France as Irish airfields would not meet German requirements. The conclusion was that all that would be possible would be in winter months to bring occasional blockade-runners with weapons and ammunition into Irish harbours and bays, as long as there was still no state of war between Britain and Ireland and as long as the Irish co-operated.

It was rather an astonishing confession of German naval and air impotence within six months of the great German victories in the West, and while Britain was still getting over the shock of Dunkirk and suffering crippling blows from the submarine warfare. Nevertheless, Hitler appears to have accepted it without demur and is recorded as making the following statement about Ireland:

> A landing in Ireland can be attempted only if Ireland requests help. For the present, our envoy must ascertain whether de Valera desires support, and whether he might wish to have his military equipment supplemented by captured British war material [guns and ammunition] which could be sent to him on single steamers. For the C.-in-C., Air, Ireland is important as a base for attacks on the north-west ports of Britain, although weather conditions must still be investigated. The occupation of Ireland might lead to the end of war. Investigations are to be made.

On that cryptic note Hitler abandoned the Irish question and was shortly to issue the order to prepare for Operation Barbarossa, the invasion of Russia, the following June. That Hitler had no real interest in Ireland was confirmed by his deputy, Rudolf Hess, when he was being interrogated after his sensational flight to Scotland in May 1941. Sir Ivone Kirkpatrick told the Nuremberg war crimes court: 'I then threw a fly over him [Hess] about Ireland. He said that in all his talks with Hitler, the subject of Ireland had never been mentioned except incidentally. Ireland had done nothing for Germany in this war and it was therefore to be supposed that Hitler would not concern himself in Anglo-Irish relations. We had some little conversation about the difficulties of reconciling the wishes of the South and the North and from this we passed to American interest in Ireland and so to America.'

Following Hitler's naval conference, Ribbentrop continued to urge Hempel to get de Valera's reaction to the proposal to supply captured British war material. This was an impressive 46 field guns, 550 machine-guns, 10,000 rifles, 1,000 anti-tank rifles, all with the necessary ammunition. It made the British trickle of arms supplies to the Irish army look miserly, but de Valera and his advisers realised the danger of taking up the German offer. Hempel himself soon came to realise that the German offer was an embarrassment for the Irish government. He was unable to see de Valera himself before Christmas as the latter's eye ailment had become worse and he had to go into hospital, but he let Hempel know through Walshe that he saw no possibility of shipping the weapons unnoticed to Ireland as if the plan was discovered the British would immediately assert the existence of a German-Irish plot. So the Irish government had no other recourse but to abandon the acquisition of arms 'until a British attack, which was unlikely for the time being, had become a fact'. Ribbentrop was annoyed and made Hempel take it up again with de Valera early in 1941 while hinting that Irish resistance to a British attack could hardly be all it was being made out to be if they would not accept German arms in advance. With a touch of humour, which Hempel seemed to appreciate, de Valera said that the German General Staff, even without Irish participation, would presumably with German thoroughness take the measures that seemed to it appropriate in the event of a British attack. And there the matter ended.

Before this polite but firm impasse had been reached, however, the Germans had made a diplomatic blunder in the week before Christmas in proposing to send a Luftwaffe plane to Ireland with extra personnel for the legation. In November, General Warlimont had made a passing reference to the sending of some civilian meteorologists to Ireland, and the question had also come up of sending 'an official or officer experienced in military reconnaissance' to the legation in Dublin. Hitler's desire for more information about the situation in Ireland may have given the matter new urgency as Hempel suddenly told Boland of the proposal to bring the new staff in by German plane to the aerodrome at Rineanna, which is today Shannon Airport. The plane was to arrive in a few days time on Christmas Eve. Boland recalls that he told Hempel that this request could only be granted by the government and he did not think it would be. Hempel became agitated and said it was the first request Germany had made and it was being refused. The situation was especially delicate as de Valera had just gone into hospital.

Lt-General Dan McKenna, who was the Irish Chief of Staff, still had a vivid memory of the episode thirty-two years later. He recalled being at lunch in Hempel's residence in Monkstown on Tuesday, 17 December, and the German minister drawing him aside afterwards – 'he practically pushed me by the shoulders into a corner' – and impressing on him that he had no need whatever to fear a German invasion. Later that day McKenna began a tour of military installations in the north, but the next day he was recalled urgently to Dublin where the Minister for Defence, Mr Oscar Traynor, was waiting for him. The meeting took place in the early hours of Thursday morning and went as follows. Traynor said ominously: 'It's happened.' McKenna asked: 'Which side is it?' and Traynor answered: 'the Germans'.

McKenna said that Traynor had told him that Hempel had gone to see the Deputy Prime Minister, Mr Sean T. O'Kelly (presumably after being rebuffed by Boland) who, to Hempel's indignation, also stalled on the proposal. It was decided to inform de Valera in hospital and he is said to have ordered the immediate arrest of the Germans if they landed at Rineanna (which would have had to be cleared of obstacles to permit a landing). A general alert of the defence forces was ordered and Maj-General Costello, in charge of the southern forces, was given the job of arresting the Germans. General McKenna says that on the morning of Christmas Eve a German plane actually did fly in low over Rineanna but flew away again. For him it was the biggest scare of the emergency period. Many other men who were in the army at that time recalled Christmas 1940 as one of great tension but are convinced that it was because of the threat of a *British* invasion and nothing will convince them that it was not. (The Catholic Bishop of Derry, Dr Farren, did send de Valera a message around this time that a British soldier in a bar in Derry had been boasting about crossing the border and de Valera passed it on to Colonel Archer of army intelligence but it was not taken seriously.)

The war cabinet meeting on 23 December, the day before the Luftwaffe plane was due in Ireland, was told by the new Dominions Secretary, Lord Cranborne, that Maffey had reported a 'change of heart' by the Irish and that Walshe had proposed that Cranborne should go to Dublin. 'It seems,' the cabinet was told, 'that the German Minister in Dublin had offended the Irish.'

Hempel and de Valera had it out at a lively confrontation on 27 December with Hempel vigorously emphasising the 'gravity of the situation' and de Valera calmly explaining the rationale of Irish neutrality. Hempel retorted that he remained within his instructions and he 'did not speak about possible concrete consequences of a negative Irish attitude either'. Senior army officers believed they saw these 'consequences' when German bombs fell in the first two days of 1941 near Drogheda, in Counties Wexford, Carlow (three killed), Wicklow, Kildare and twice in Dublin itself injuring twenty-four persons. The last German bombing had been the previous August when a creamery at Campile, Co Wexford, had been destroyed and three girls killed. The new year spate of bombings may not have been connected with the affair of the extra legation staff but it was a curious coincidence at the very least.

Notes to this chapter are on p 180

Chapter 5

The Economic Squeeze

When Churchill made his House of Commons speech at the beginning of November 1940 putting a large share of the blame for the huge shipping losses on Ireland for refusing to hand over the Atlantic ports, he was harping on an old grievance and, as we saw in the previous chapter, the British Press picked up the familiar scent in full cry. The war cabinet was told that public opinion was becoming rapidly inflamed. A stream of embarrassing parliamentary questions demanding to know how the government intended to bring the ungrateful Irish to heel were being tabled, and it was with difficulty that the indignant MPs were persuaded to withdraw them by the Dominions Secretary, Lord Cranborne who was getting alarming reports from Maffey in Dublin on the Irish fears of an impending British invasion.

When Cranborne tried to draw Churchill's attention to the unforeseen sequel to his verbal broadside, the latter was unmoved and he fired off a typical reply:

> I think it would be better to let de Valera stew in his own juice for a while . . . The claim now put forward on behalf of de Valera is that we are not only to be strangled by them, but to suffer our fate without making any complaint. Sir John Maffey should be made aware of the rising anger in England and Scotland and especially among the merchant seamen, and he should not be encouraged to think that his only task is to mollify de Valera and make everything, including our ruin, pass off pleasantly.[1]

If Churchill really believed that the terrible toll of merchant shipping could largely be attributed to Irish neutrality, then his anger and bitterness were understandable but not necessarily justified. In a speech in the House of Commons on 5 May 1938, when he was the only MP to oppose the recent agreement to hand back the ports, Churchill foresaw just such an eventuality:

> The ports may be denied us in the hour of need, and we may be hampered in the gravest manner in protecting the British population from privation and even starvation . . . It will be no use saying, 'Then we will retake the ports.' You will have no right to do so. To violate Irish neutrality should it be declared at the moment of a Great War may put you out of court in the opinion of the world, and may vitiate the cause by which you may be involved in war.

When he became First Lord of the Admiralty fifteen months later on the outbreak of war, Churchill, as we have seen, tried to wriggle out of this dilemma by arguing that Irish neutrality was 'illegal' and need not be respected. But the bulldog's bark was worse than his bite and when he did assume the supreme office, he was able to restrain himself from the rash action he had warned against in 1938. What he could not know in 1940, as it was only revealed after years of sifting through captured German records, was that the Germans had cracked the Royal Navy's secret codes as far back as 1936 when the British fleet was stationed in the Red Sea to implement the League economic sanctions against Italy for her annexation of Abyssinia. Donald McLachlan, who worked in naval intelligence during the war comments in his book *Room 39*: 'True, this tragic and shocking failure of signal security had been completely overcome by the summer of 1943; but for nearly four critical years Admiral Doenitz reaped a rich harvest of sunken supply ships – $11\frac{1}{2}$ million tons in the North Atlantic alone.'

But at the close of 1940 neutral Ireland was the villain in Churchill's eyes and he was determined to teach her a lesson. He bombarded the Chancellor of the Exchequer, Sir Kingsley Wood, with memoranda urging him to devise a scheme to cut off the agricultural subsidies on Irish imports, apparently under the false impression that these imports were heavily subsidised. Churchill was afraid of the possible unfavourable reaction in the United States where Roosevelt was lobbying hard for a change in the Neutrality Act to permit him to bring in the lease-lend system to help Britain. In a letter to Roosevelt on 13 December

1940, Churchill told him that Britain could no longer carry the 400,000 tons of feeding-stuffs and fertilisers which they had conveyed to Eire through enemy attacks and the cabinet proposed telling de Valera of this. 'He will of course have plenty of food for his own people, but they will not have the prosperous trading they are making now.'[2] Churchill asked for Roosevelt's reaction to this move, which he was careful not to portray as a policy of economic sanctions, and added that Britain was also thinking of withdrawing the agricultural subsidies as merchant seamen and public opinion were taking it 'much amiss that we should have to carry Irish supplies through air and U-Boat attacks and subsidise them handsomely when de Valera is quite content to sit happily and see us strangled'.

Working at commendable speed Kingsley Wood had two plans prepared for economic pressure on Ireland to present to the war cabinet on 6 December, only twenty-four hours after Churchill had demanded action. The first plan would make the population 'feel uncomfortable in a few weeks' and the second one would be the equivalent of 'economic war'.[3]

The first item dealt with was shipping. The chancellor explained that there was 'an unwritten understanding' that Eire chartered ships through the Minister of Shipping's Charter Office (he did not say that Ireland had done this to oblige Britain who had complained that competition between them was pushing up the charter rates for neutral ships). Eire also got space in liners and other ships chartered to Britain, and Irish needs in both kinds of shipping space was estimated at the equivalent of forty whole-time ships. Eire was already feeling the pinch with the reduction of the second kind of shipping space, and the chancellor now proposed to tell the Ministry of Shipping no longer to give Eire any charter facilities whatever. In addition, the Greeks and Norwegians were to be told they should not charter ships 'except to Allies or co-operators'. The result would be 'that Eire might get if she were very lucky, 10 ships, which would give her 25 per cent of her needs'.

The next item on the plan was commodities. The chancellor proposed that the export licensing arrangements should be altered so as to shut out the export or re-export to Eire of food, feeding-stuffs and fertilisers, agricultural and other machinery, spare parts of all kinds, iron and steel, non-ferrous metals, chemical and electrical goods, paper and cardboard. 'Small exceptions might be made, for instance in the case of tea on which the Irish could be cut to something below the English ration.' This would deprive Eire almost entirely of space in ships bringing goods to the United Kingdom, he observed.

With coal a different situation obtained as Eire took some 3 million tons a year which gave employment to about 10,000 miners. Also, as there was an export drive in coal as well as cotton goods and textiles, Britain would 'not have the same ground for starving Eire as in the commodities previously mentioned'.

The second plan would be in effect economic war, the chancellor explained, because the Minister for Shipping could withhold facilities for the insurance of ships going to Eire 'and this would mean that they would get no ships'. The effect on Eire would be drastic shortages and a profound psychological shock. Britain would lose exports of some £24 million a year but as they would be in the same currency the short-term economic effect would not be serious except possibly for the miners in South Wales. Eire might retaliate by expropriating Guinness and the National Stud (later in the war Britain removed all the breeding stock after a lengthy legal wrangle and only then did the Irish government nationalise it).

The war cabinet was told by Cranborne that he favoured the first plan, but excluding action on coal and dollars. The Chiefs of Staff had to consider the eventuality of Ireland ceding to the economic pressure and handing over the bases. They were clearly unprepared for the commitment to defend Ireland against German air or land attacks, a commitment which had been so freely promised by MacDonald, Maffey and Churchill.[4] Thus if Britain got the bases with Ireland's consent the Chiefs of Staff estimated that the defence of the country would require 288 heavy and 318 light anti-aircraft guns, 312 searchlights, 6 fighter squadrons with facilities for 24. Ireland's chances of getting adequate anti-aircraft protection can be judged by the plight of Belfast the following April and May when there was little or no resistance either on the ground or in the air to the German bombers which inflicted just under 1,000 fatal casualties, damaged 56,000 houses and hammered the shipyards.

The Chiefs of Staff also made the interesting calculation that if the ports were taken over by force it would require ten British divisions to keep control of the country. Incidentally, senior Irish army officers who should know say that this figure was deliberately inflated by British staff officers friendly to Ireland (such as General Alanbrooke, later Chief of the Imperial General Staff, who himself came from north Irish stock) to discourage Churchill from rashly deciding on an Irish invasion.

Although the economic plan was ready to swing into action, Churchill hesitated throughout December because there was no answer from Roosevelt to his tentative soundings and apparently no answer came. At the war cabinet meeting on 2 January 1941 it was decided to go ahead with the first plan which meant that export licences would in future be required for the export to Ireland of the goods mentioned previously and 'such Licences will then be withheld at the instance of the Departments severally concerned. No major decision of His Majesty's Government need be announced.' The Ministry of Food might be under some obligation, the Chancellor of the Exchequer explained, to allow the shipment to Eire of consignments which it had brought to Britain as the agent of the Irish government and which were technically the property of the Irish government. This was probably a reference to tea as Ireland had agreed to import it through the British Tea Control on the understanding she would get her normal requirements.

The chancellor added that the Ministry of Shipping 'will find itself unable to fix ships for Eire without, for the moment, making any official announcement'. Later when the ministry had safely got control of all available Norwegian and Greek ships, it would 'release' Eire from her undertaking to charter only through Britain. The Norwegians and Greeks would be told that they must not charter any of their free ships to Eire.

Churchill seemed satisfied and told the cabinet that when the Irish government was informed of what they proposed, 'it should be emphasised that this step was taken in no vindictive spirit and only dire necessity had forced us into such a step'. It was also agreed that the Ministry of Information should inform the Press that 'the Government viewed this measure with profound regret'.

Perhaps there was some consolation for the Irish government in the cabinet's decision to allow any Eire or neutral ships engaged in Eire trade to receive the protection of British convoys (Irish ships later stopped sailing in convoys when they found they were being assigned to the more dangerous outside places). Another consolation – which was not to be divulged, however – was that the policy in regard to the regulation of food supplies to Eire should be one of 'gradual diminution' and so tea supplies should not be cut off all at once but continued in 'small quantities' for the present.

The war cabinet would have found it much more difficult, if not impossible, to embark on this disguised economic sanctions campaign at this time if the Anglo-Irish Trade Agreement which it had authorised the previous 19 August had been duly signed. But the Irish government, which had taken the initiative to open the talks in London in April 1940, refused at the last minute to sign the agreement thus unwittingly giving Churchill a free hand to put on the economic squeeze. The Irish public was never told of the government's refusal to sign this agreement and when opposition spokesmen from time to time in the Dail criticised the government for not having made some contractual arrangement with Britain to ensure a minimum of essential suppies in exchange for farm produce, the ministers concerned used to reply evasively implying that Britain's attitude had been the main obstacle.

The talks which began on 30 April 1940 lasted for a week with Ireland represented by the Minister for Supplies, Mr Lemass, and the Minister for Agriculture, Dr Ryan.[5] The British side was led by Anthony Eden who was still Dominions Secretary. The talks had broken down on the prices which Britain was offering for butter, cheese and bacon. According to the British confidential report (nothing of substance ever appeared in the Irish newspapers) Lemass and Ryan said that these prices would put Irish farmers out of production and they went back to Dublin.

The British agreed that the prices were too low but said they were based on those for imports from the other Dominions where production costs were lower. They proposed to the Irish that the difference could be made up by the price paid for fat cattle imports which would be the equivalent of a £500,000 annual subsidy. By August, Caldecote, the new Dominions Secretary, had persuaded the war cabinet to accept these terms and the Irish High Commissioner, Dulanty, was pressing for an answer. But now the Irish balked again and this time over the clause giving Britain storage, port and trans-shipment facilities which the Ministry of Shipping was welcoming as a way of relieving congestion in British ports.

In November the war cabinet was told that Eire had rejected the storage and trans-shipment proposals as being incompatible with neutrality and from fears that they would provoke German attacks on the ports if not on the country as a whole. The Irish government also wanted assurances, not previously offered, in regard to the provision of shipping and insurance of shipping for the Eire trade and the rates to be paid for that shipping. Ireland's refusal of the trade agreement may have left her vulnerable to the British economic pressure, but the refusal also sealed off a potential serious breach in Ireland's neutrality and nothing was more important for de Valera.

After the new economic measures had been in force for three months, the war cabinet was given a progress report by the Dominions Secretary, Lord Cranborne. Only enough coal was being allowed to be shipped to Ireland to keep the Cork gasworks going without any reserve stocks, and no fats, sugar or wheat were being shipped at all. The general view in the cabinet was that the present policy should in no way be relaxed. It was 'consistent with our needs and ostensibly it should continue to be based on those needs. At the same time it was important from the political view that the pressure on Eire should be fully maintained.'[6]

But the most interesting aspect of this meeting by far was a long secret memorandum which Cranborne had drawn up on 19 March 1941, summarising the effects on Ireland of the new economic policy and one extract gives a good idea of its flavour.[7]

> Its main object, it will be remembered, was to open the eyes of the Irish people to their true situation. Since the outbreak of war they had been living in a world of illusion. They thought that their products and their goodwill were essential to Great Britain, and that she could not afford to let them go short, much less to quarrel with them. They therefore sat comfortably back and submitted to the delicious process of being spoon-fed. They were confident that, if they became short of any commodity, the British Navy would convoy fresh supplies safely into their harbours. They need themselves do nothing. As a neutral, they would enjoy the protection which neutrality gives. As a member of the British Commonwealth, they could claim the special advantages which such membership confers; and they could do so without any unpleasant feeling of gratitude to the hated Englishman. If Britain were helping Ireland, she was not doing it from any noble motive, but because it paid her. It was a very happy situation, and they saw no reason why it should not continue indefinitely.
>
> It can at any rate be claimed of the new policy that it has brought that

frame of mind to an end. The bubble of Irish complacency has effectively and we may hope finally been pricked. The Southern Irish now know that England is not dependent on them and that on the contrary, it is Ireland that is dependent on England . . . To-day Southern Ireland is very uncomfortable, and she is going to become progressively more uncomfortable. But for this she is not able to blame us. The blame rests, first on Germany and secondly on herself. It is a direct result of her policy of neutrality.

By now the reader will have probably realised that the neutrality issue was not quite as simple as that and one suspects that Cranborne's deliberately simplistic view and moral indignation covered an underlying guilty conscience at this bullying of a small country into a war in which she would be defenceless against the aerial blitz then devastating British cities. Cranborne also exaggerated the sense of complacency in Ireland by the end of 1940. De Valera and other ministers were ceaselessly declaiming about the peril which confronted the country and the one in four of the male population between eighteen and sixty-four enrolled for defence in a full- or part-time capacity was the equivalent of 10 million men in the United States or 3 million in the United Kingdom.

Cranborne was right that the new year 1941 brought a rude shock for the Irish government and people alike on the question of supplies. The first shock came at Christmas when the petrol pumps all over the country ran dry and motorists were stranded in large numbers as they tried to make their way back to Dublin after the holiday. The three main British distributors had informed their Irish subsidiaries that petrol supplies might be cut off completely and the government reacted by forbidding petrol sales temporarily to check stocks. When sales resumed, however, the ration for private motorists was reduced by three-quarters. Coal was cut to half a ton a month and later disappeared altogether for domestic use. The biggest blow was in tea which had been freely available before the squeeze. In January 1941 a ration of 2oz a week was introduced but at the beginning of April it was reduced to 1oz and a few days later this meagre ration was halved. The cutting off of wheat imports meant the end of white bread and the 90 per cent wheat extraction loaf was accepted with bad grace in Ireland. It was little consolation to read that the 90 per cent wheat loaf was praised by English dieticians for its nutritional value – they hadn't got to eat it! The situation in Ireland was made even more depressing by the out-

F

" He says he's goin' to make damn sure he doesn't miss next week's train ! '

Dublin Opinion *view of the transport difficulties.*

break of foot and mouth disease which halted cattle exports to Britain. Wild rumours circulated that the Germans were responsible and Limerick County Council voted to intern gypsies while the outbreak lasted and even made threatening noises about rural postmen. The army had the lugubrious task of shooting the stricken beasts and burying them. More than 19,000 cattle and 5,000 sheep were destroyed. The army, incidentally, had also been commandeered earlier in the emergency to feed the elephants in the Dublin Zoo when the farmers' strike cut off their supplies of fodder.[8]

It was only to be expected, then, that when the Dail debated the supplies situation in April and June 1941, Mr Lemass should come in for heavy criticism from opposition members who were unaware of the real reason for the sudden shortages. In spite of Cranborne's claim that the economic squeeze had been put on without giving the Irish any grounds for 'valid suspicion' that it was deliberate, the game was given away, as far as Lemass was concerned, by the tea anomaly. He pointed out that while Ireland had been cut to 25 per cent of her normal requirements or to 500,000lb a year, Britain, which normally consumed 400 million lb a year, was on an 85 per cent ration. Lemass said meaningfully: 'I do not propose to speculate here as to the possible real explanation of this rapid restriction in our tea supply, but it is clear that the explanation that has been given to us is inadequate.'[9] Soon afterwards he was vigorously denying that he had attributed any unworthy motive to Britain for imposing these shortages. Three years later in 1944 he was to hint in the Dail that the tea cuts had been due to 'pressure by British trade interests'. The opposition remained blissfully unaware of the real reason for the shortages and when coal imports were virtually suspended in 1944 (this time because of the D-Day preparations), Mr John A. Costello of Fine Gael, who was to lead the later coalition governments, berated Lemass and his colleagues saying that if they had gone over to London 'they could have got as much coal as they wanted from Great Britain because Great Britain has treated us very generously for the past three or four years'.

Thrown back brutally on their own fairly meagre resources, the de Valera government got down vigorously to the job of ensuring economic as well as political survival. The doctrine of self-sufficiency which it had introduced during the economic war period of the mid-thirties and which had been denounced by Fine Gael, now proved to have been invaluable and the little leather and textile factories kept the country shod and clothed throughout the war. The switch from grazing to tillage which Fianna Fail had also encouraged was now stepped up and under the goad of compulsory orders, the farmers increased the pre-war tillage area by one million acres with the most spectacular increase being in wheat which jumped from 21,000 acres in 1932 to 230,000 in 1938 and 640,000 in 1944.

Strenuous efforts were made to substitute native turf for the now scarce British coal and Dublin's Phoenix Park became disfigured by towering ricks of turf stretching for several miles. Dubliners were encouraged to cut their own turf from the bogs in the mountains south of the city and the army was inevitably pressed into service as turf cutters. A scheme to recruit the Dublin unemployed for this worthy

Ingenious turf-poachers in the Phœnix Park.

Dublin Opinion *view of the fuel shortage.*

cause had little success as the dropout rate after one day was 50 per cent. The coal cuts did not merely mean colder grates, but it drastically affected the transport services – not just the trains but the Dublin trams also as most of the capital's electricity was generated by coal. The quality as well as the quantity of the coal which Britain was supplying deteriorated rapidly and the 'chaotic' situation which hit the rail network in September 1941 was described in picturesque terms in the Dail by a parliamentary secretary, Mr Hugo Flinn, who said: 'We had cases where a couple of hundred of empty waggons were sent off and simply did not arrive at their destinations. You had passenger trains which went out into the blue and remained in the blue. The end of it was that by the middle of October the railways had practically sat down, due to the amount and quality of coal.'

The sudden curtailment of the supply of vital raw materials was a severe blow for a small island country in a war zone and with few natural resources of its own. The government made a bold effort to meet the challenge by setting up the Scientific Research Bureau in February 1941 headed by four scientists and an engineer from the universities. The latter, Dr A. M. Hogan, had been borrowed temporarily by the British government earlier in the war to advise on safety measures for mines.[10]

Eighteen months later Mr de Valera gave the Dail a progress report on the work being carried out by the Scientific Research Bureau and his detailed description of thirteen experiments which were being conducted showed some notable successes.[11]

The biggest achievement was probably the building up of an ocean-going Irish shipping line in face of tremendous difficulties. The Fianna Fail government must also take the major responsibility, however, in putting the country in the vulnerable position of not having one ocean-going vessel at the beginning of 1941 when Britain suddenly withdrew the joint charter service. In spite of its self-sufficiency philosophy, Fianna Fail had a curious blind-spot where the sea was concerned. An effort had been made to set up a proper Irish merchant marine before the war, but foreign interests were able to crush it by temporarily lowering shipping rates and something similar happened to Lemass's attempt to build an oil refinery at Dublin port (a project which was revived in 1972 to the anguish of the environmentalists). With the all-embracing emergency powers, however, the government could certainly have been making provision from the outbreak of the war for the kind of shipping crisis which burst in 1941 by such a simple expedient as buying the occasional ship to have in reserve.

Because of the oil-refinery project, Ireland had probably the most modern oil-tanker fleet in the world when the war broke out as Lord Inverforth had arranged to have seven tankers built in Germany with frozen marks in 1938 for the Dublin refinery. The tankers, totalling 97,400 tons deadweight were owned by Inver Tankers Ltd, an English company which itself was owned by Messrs Andrew Weir & Co, but they were registered in Ireland. The files now available in the Public Record Office show that when the refinery project hung fire, Lord Inverforth thought of selling the tankers to Japan, but with the impending war the British government put strong pressure on him not to sell abroad and the Irish government were asked if they would requisition the ships for use by Britain. The Irish government replied that it would be against their policy to requisition the ships but offered to transfer them to the British register. When war broke out the transfer duly took place on 6 September 1939 and the British files note that 'the Eire Government attached no conditions of any kind to the transfer of flag and were most helpful and gave every assistance in securing the use of the ships for His Majesty's Government'.[12] Needless to say this helpfulness was bitterly regretted when Britain cut Ireland's normal petroleum supply of 250,000 tons by half in 1941, and cut the previous year's allotment by a quarter in 1942 and 1943. The 1943 reduction drew a strong protest from the Irish High Commissioner, J. W. Dulanty in a letter of 23 February 1943:

> My Government has been forced to the conclusion that the proposals in your letter regarding provision for Ireland for 1943 are not only harsh and inequitable. In view of the understanding arrived at between the two countries at the beginning of the war and before the transfer of the seven tankers from the Irish Register to the British Register, they must be regarded as little short of a breach of faith. In the circumstances my Government regret that they have no choice left to them, if the proposals are persisted in, but to request the immediate return to the Irish Register of tanker tonnage equivalent to the aggregate tonnage.

The British government, as we have seen, maintained that the tankers were handed over unconditionally and besides they were British owned; but Clement Attlee, who was Dominions Secretary at this time, sympathised with the Irish plight and in a memo suggested to his colleagues that: 'Nevertheless, it is the case that in agreeing without difficulty to the transfer of the tankers in September 1939, the Irish acquired some claim to special consideration in the sphere of oil supplies.' But the other members of the War Cabinet Committee on Economic Policy towards Eire overruled Attlee's suggestion that the 1943 cut of 25 per cent be revoked, and Dulanty's threat of claiming equivalent tanker tonnage was of course an ineffective one.

Putting their mistakes behind them, the government decided in February 1941 to establish a deep-sea fleet and in March Irish Shipping Ltd was incorporated under the chairmanship of John Leydon, Secretary of the Department of Supplies and the man who had gone to London a few days before the war started to discuss the maintenance of full supplies of coal and raw materials. Irish Shipping consisted of representatives of the three existing Irish shipping companies and of Grain Importers (Eire) Ltd. The companies supplied the professional expertise but at a later stage the government acquired all the shares.[13]

In spite of the world shortage and the high prices, Irish Shipping bought eight vessels and chartered five in its first year and they were all renamed after trees. The fleet eventually totalled fifteen ships but the loss of the two chartered American liberty ships, the *Irish Oak* and the *Irish Pine* in 1942-3 represented 20 per cent of carrying capacity. By the end of the war, Irish Shipping had carried just over one million tons of cargo to Ireland of which wheat alone accounted for two-thirds. The company also branched into maritime insurance and made it a highly profitable business. In all, twenty Irish ships were lost at a cost of 138 lives but the heaviest losses were among the small coasters which daringly took on the Dublin–Lisbon–Dublin run and in some cases even went south as far as West Africa. Under the navicert system as operated by the British Ministry of Economic Warfare, all Irish ships had to call at British ports on the inward and outward run to have cargoes checked. Attacks on these unarmed little ships by German aircraft were frequent but in the case of the *Kerlogue* it was an RAF plane. When the Irish government used to protest to the German government the reply often was that no responsibility could be taken as the ships had been in the German blockade zone through which Irish ships had been offered free passage but on terms which were rejected. Blockaded Ireland owed an immense debt to her merchant seamen in those years, but they have received little enough recognition for their vital services.

The informal committee under the Dominions Secretary, which had been assigned by Churchill in 1941 to the task of keeping up the economic pressure on Ireland, was reconstructed as a full war cabinet committee early in 1942 under Attlee.

Only some of the committee's business can be described here. One interesting, if pathetic, feature which the committee's file reveals is that Ireland's whole source of pressure when the going got rough was the the threat to withhold supplies of Guinness. Early in 1942 the Irish government proposed an exchange of beer for wheat, but this was rejected as the British had to keep up the pretence that the squeeze on Ireland was due to genuine shortages and the principle of barter was thus ruled out. But the Minister of Food, Lord Woolton, then received the news that Eire was stopping the export of beer altogether and he was alarmed at the effect on Northern Ireland which got 80 per cent of its beer supplies from the south. He minuted: 'The effect of this on the output of essential works in Belfast and other places will I fear be serious.' He urged that Britain offer Eire not more than 30,000 tons of wheat in exchange for an undertaking to maintain the full 1941 rate of beer exports of one million barrels. In fact the Irish negotiators were not tough enough and only got 20,000 tons of wheat. The American minister in Dublin, David Gray, got to hear of the deal and was quite annoyed and protested to Maffey: 'This is not what the American Government is urging Americans to make sacrifices for. A further weakness, in the American view, is that it exchanges a vital necessity for what Americans regard at the best as a luxury and at worst as a poison.' Guinnesses would not have been flattered.

The committee's general policy was defined at one stage as 'keeping Eire's economy going on a minimum basis'. It was never, therefore, starvation but a question of constantly reminding the Irish that they owed their survival to Britain but had refused to pull their weight and so must expect to pay some price in personal comfort. In any case, apart from tea and white bread the Irish were better fed than the British with meat, bacon, butter and eggs always fairly plentiful for those who could afford them. Even tea was never in practice restricted to the official half ounce as the middle classes had stocked up well in advance of the real scarcity and the usual black market flourished.

Shortly after the war ended, a New Zealand minister called Sullivan visited Dublin to arrange for diplomatic representation. Maffey reported back to London that de Valera told Sullivan that Irish feeling towards Britain was good for two reasons: first, admiration for British courage during the war and second, because of the 'fair way' Britain had treated Ireland on supplies.[14]

An odd counterpoint to the economic pressure campaign against Ireland was the obsession in certain quarters of the Foreign Office in London with the state of Catholic and clerical opinion in Dublin regarding the war and the efforts which were made to influence such opinion in a pro-allied direction. We have already seen how Cardinal McRory early in the war was put on the Ministry of Information's mailing list, but there must have been deep disillusionment at the increasingly visible failure to persuade the cardinal to moderate his outspoken anti-partitionist views and scarcely concealed anti-British attitude. Dublin also worried about the cardinal and a senior minister, Mr Sean T. O'Kelly, was sent to cool him down.

The Foreign Office fully supported the scheme by the Ministry of Information to send over to Dublin a stream of distinguished visitors ostensibly to lecture on Catholic subjects but in reality to work on influential opinion in Ireland to favour the allied cause. One of these visitors was Count Balinski of the Polish Research Centre whose family had historical links with Ireland. In the course of a fortnight in January 1941 the count gave a series of lectures and met a large number of leading figures in the political and cultural spheres including de Valera who 'indicated great interest in the effects of the German occupation of Poland'. The count found the new Catholic Archbishop of Dublin, Dr McQuaid and the Papal Nuncio Monsignor Paschal Robinson 'well acquainted with the facts of religious persecution carried on by the Germans and the Russians'. The Irish Jesuits, he was happy to observe, showed 'very decided pro-British feelings'.[15]

The Catholic weekly newspaper the *Standard* was, according to the count, the 'only very decidedly anti-British and isolationist paper' and from a conversation with the editor, Mr Peter O'Curry, he got the impression that 'it caters deliberately for people with insular tendencies.' The *Standard* in 1942 won a libel action against the *Daily Mail* for an article by an American journalist which alleged the paper was 'pro-Axis in its editorial policy, that it was fed with Axis propaganda and that it was the organ of a group that would rather see Germany than England win the war'. On the censorship policy, Count Balinski reported that it was severely criticised by the Irish themselves and that its severity could not be justified by the neutrality policy. He said that nothing was published which showed the spirit of the British people in their struggle or about the Vatican Radio broadcasts on the persecution of the Catholic church in Poland and Germany.

The Foreign Office was pleased with the count's report and urged that more such visits be organised, perhaps using Dutch and Norwegian spokesmen. It was soon after this that the decision was made to send over John Betjeman (now Sir John and Poet Laureate) to Dublin as a press attaché in Maffey's office. One of his chief duties was to persuade the Irish that the German 'new order' was anti-Christian, but he reported in March 1941 that he found 'even among the most sincere Catholics a refusal to believe in stories of German persecution'. Part of the trouble was the Irish people with long memories remembered how allied propaganda about German atrocities in World War I were shown afterwards to be false. Betjeman also had trouble with the *Standard* which he described as 'most tendentious and difficult. Its chief lines are that the Catholics in the North are persecuted – which is true and a sure sales getter – and that the war is one of big business.' The *Standard*, Betjeman continued, maintained that of the two 'belligerents' Germany had less big business than Britain because she did more for the unemployed and therefore it would be better if Germany won. Betjeman said he had made friends with the editor and was trying to show him that Germany was anti-Christian. He advised London that it would help his job if the Catholic paper the *Universe* and *Picture Post* published straightforward illustrated articles of the persecution of Polish Catholics by the Nazis.[16]

Notes to this chapter are on p 181

Chapter 6

The War Gets Nearer

On the evening of 2 January 1941, the assistant naval attaché in the British embassy in Belgrade was urgently summoned to the office of the acting director of military intelligence of the Yugoslav armed forces. The naval attaché reported back to London that he was closely questioned about the state of British defences in Ireland and the views of southern Ireland towards Germany. The report concluded that the Yugoslav 'refused to state he had any information definitely as to impending German attack on Ireland but no doubt was conveying this impression from information he had probably received in confidence'. In London the Naval Intelligence Department passed on the report to the Foreign Office with the comment: 'This may well be the war of nerves technique', a view which the latter endorsed pointing out that the Germans had just publicly stated that they had discovered a British 'plot' to invade Ireland.[1]

The combination of the clumsy German attempts to compromise Irish neutrality by pressing the offer of captured British arms, the tension caused by the episode to increase the German legation staff, the German air raids and the German attempts to whip up an invasion scare, seems to have caused de Valera to make a definite pro-British shift in policy around this time. The American minister, David Gray, reported to Washington on 25 January 1941 that de Valera had told him that 'he was convinced that the Germans would invade Ireland and he intended to tell the Cabinet to face this situation realistically'.[2] Another influential factor was Churchill's economic pressure campaign which in a matter of weeks had brought home to de Valera and his ministers the country's dependence on British goodwill for essential supplies of petroleum, coal, wheat and other imported foodstuffs.

As a price for such a rapprochement, de Valera proposed to Maffey that Britain should give a guarantee not to invade Ireland, but Churchill, who had already rejected such a proposal received privately from the deputy leader of the Fine Gael opposition party, Mr James Dillon, also turned down de Valera's. Maffey explained to him that if the Germans ever forced them into a tight corner, they had to be free to take whatever measures were necessary and the time might come when Britain or America, or both, would have to put pressure on Ireland.[3]

It was four days after Maffey's frank interview with de Valera that the Irish Chief of Staff, Lt-General McKenna, had an important meeting on 18 March with Brigadier Gregson-Ellis from Northern Ireland which resulted in the existing liaison arrangements for combined resistance in the event of a German invasion of the south being greatly developed and strengthened. The original Irish enthusiasm for such a liaison, which had brought Lt-Colonel Dudley Clarke over to Dublin in May 1940, had quickly cooled as a result of the failure of the Malcolm MacDonald mission and the hostile British Press campaign hinting at a 'defence pact' to de Valera's great embarrassment. The Major Byass affair had not helped relations either. As a result, the Irish army staff remained aloof and although the British forces in the north were more or less ready to come south in the event of a German invasion, the joint planning for such a move did not really exist in the second half of 1940.

The meeting between McKenna and Gregson-Ellis, the chief staff officer of General Sir Harold Franklyn who commanded British Troops Northern Ireland (BTNI), must have been authorised by de Valera as General McKenna told the author that he always reported personally to de Valera after each meeting with British staff officers. One of McKenna's staff officers was Bobby Childers, a son of Erskine Childers who had been executed by the Free State Government during the Civil War, and a brother of President Childers. Childers was able to arrange that 'Annamoe', the beautiful Co Wicklow home of the Barton family who were related to the Childers, was available for discreet meetings between General McKenna and General Franklyn.

The liaison between the two staffs, which now entered on an active phase lasting until 1944 when a German invasion threat was no longer feasible, centred on the W plan which co-ordinated the rapid British advance from the north with the first resistance of Irish troops to a German landing in the extreme south. Elaborate efforts were taken by both governments after the war to conceal the fact that such co-operation had taken place, as we have seen in the case of the censoring of Dudley Clarke's book. The Northern Ireland government, for its part, distrusted this cross-border co-operation in defence matters but BTNI, which was a distinct command from the garrison troops of Northern Ireland District, came directly under the War Office and ignored any political objections made by the Stormont Government by appealing directly to London.

In June 1940 there was only the 53rd Division available in Northern Ireland to resist a German invasion in the south, and a brigade of Royal Marines was concentrated at Milford Haven to be ready to seize a bridgehead in Eire if the Germans landed. Reinforcements arrived in the north in the shape of the 61st Infantry Division, but Churchill criticised the length of time taken to transport a unit of this size across the Irish Sea and urged that smaller units be used for swift movement pointing out that they would probably not need heavy artillery against lightly armed German paratroops. In July 1940 the 148th Infantry Brigade Group moved to the north and early in 1941 it was followed by the 71st and 72nd Brigades and finally the 5th Division, making four divisions in all.[4]

If the Germans landed in the south and the Irish government requested help (this was to be done through Maffey who had a radio set, but in the last resort carrier pigeons were on standby), the 53rd Division would thrust south supported by the 148th Brigade and they would try to ensure reaching the Boyne (shades of King Billy) with its vital railway viaduct at Drogheda in the first hop. Equally important was the securing of Dublin and the aerodromes at Collinstown and Baldonnel where German paratroopers could have been expected. In a second phase, the British forces would advance south as fast as possible to help the Irish army which hoped to be able to hold the Germans for a minimum of forty-eight hours at their landing point. The 1st Irish Division, under Maj-General Costello and based at Cork, would bear the first brunt of the landing and the 2nd Irish Division, under Maj-General Hugo McNeill with headquarters at Carton House in Co Kildare, fifteen miles west of Dublin, would hurry south with all speed

to help Costello. Bicycle squadrons were to form an important part of
the Irish tactics to harass the Germans while waiting for British help.
The Irish army had no tanks and its armour consisted of some Bren-gun
carriers and armoured cars of civil war vintage and a few built by the
Ford factory in Cork which lasted until service in the Belgian Congo
for the United Nations in 1960. The Irish resistance would be directed
by General McKenna from a field headquarters set up in a wooded spot
near Dundrum, Co Tipperary, on the northern side of the Galtee
Mountains. Some land was leased from a local lady who was unaware
that it was to serve as an airfield for supporting British fighters.

General Franklyn was to move his headquarters south to the out-
skirts of Dublin but the Grand Hotel, Malahide, which had been
chosen for him did not, for some reason, meet with his approval when
he discreetly vetted it. The main problem with which the W plan had
to cope was how to get the British forces south along narrow, twisitng
Irish roads in time to stop the Germans getting a firm foothold. When
'Zero Day' came General Franklyn's troops would cross the border in
three separate columns and converge on the Dublin area, using the
main Belfast–Dublin road along the coast, the Slane–Dublin road and
the Navan–Dublin road. A sum of £50,000 was to be available in
banks in Drogheda and Navan to pay the troops, and thousands of
small tricolour flags were to be distributed to the British forces once
they crossed the border to ensure a friendly reception from the population.[5] The Irish army had provided a railhead for the British at Fairy-
house, north of Dublin, but the real intention was not suspected as it
was also beside the racecourse where the Irish Grand National was run
every Easter Monday.

Elaborate plans were also made for the evacuation of the staffs of the
British Representative's Office and those in the trade commission, the
permit office and the war pensions office. There was some anxiety
about the fate of the five RAF wireless operators who posed as civilians
on Maffey's staff if the Germans got to Dublin and decided they were
spies. Uniforms were sent over in the diplomatic bag for this contingency. When Norman Archer on Maffey's staff informed London
that the Irish government would provide a military guard for the office
at Upper Mount Street in case there were IRA-inspired attacks on the
building when a German landing was announced, the Foreign Office
was consulted by the Dominions Office as having more experience of

this kind of thing.[6] The Foreign Office intimated that it did not favour small military guards for their missions in neutral countries because there were doubts about the efficiency and trustworthiness of such military forces. In Dublin it was possible there could be some IRA infiltrators in the guard assigned. The Dominions Office telegram to Archer continued incredibly: 'What the Foreign Office try to secure [sic] is that the office should be capable of being closed and defended against "infiltrators" by one or two sturdy messengers equipped with truncheons.' This would give time for the summoning of proper military aid or the burning of secret records.

The improved liaison between the army staffs north and south eventually eased the Irish army's shortage of modern equipment and there were frequent secret rendezvous on the border when Irish army lorries which had gone north with hams, eggs and butter returned south with badly needed military supplies. But this stage had not been reached in early 1941 when de Valera decided to make a pressing appeal to the USA for supplies, arms and ships which the British would no longer provide. In spite of traditional Irish-American links, which in the past had provided funds for the Irish struggle for independence, it was going to be difficult to win a sympathetic hearing for Irish needs in the USA at this time. Irish neutrality had irritated both Roosevelt and his minister in Dublin, David Gray, whose wife was an aunt of Mrs Roosevelt.

Gray was seventy when he was appointed by Roosevelt to be the US minister in Dublin to succeed John Cudahy who made no secret of his deep admiration for de Valera. Gray's ancestry and background did not predispose him to any excessive admiration of de Valera. His father had been born in Edinburgh and his mother was a Guthrie who were Glasgow Presbyterian divines. Gray had had an interesting and varied life before his sudden switch to diplomacy. After working for his father's paper in Buffalo, he read law and began to write fox-hunting stories. He then obtained a roving commission as a journalist in the Far East where, he told an interviewer, he 'was converted to the necessity of America's colonisation of the Philippines'. His literary output included several plays one of which, *The Best People*, was a box-office success in New York and London. During World War I he was a liaison officer with General Mangin's army in the Soissons sector in northern France. Curiously enough he later spent the year 1933-4 in

Ireland in Castletownsend in the extreme south-west where, having become extremely interested in de Valera's rise to power, he began to write a book on Ireland. But he did not finish it. In retirement after the war he wrote a new book on Ireland sharply critical of her wartime neutrality and de Valera, but he was advised by the State Department not to publish it as it contained numerous easily disproved errors relating to Irish policy in those years. At the time of his appointment to Dublin, however, Gray was reasonably open-minded.

Gray had come to Ireland in April 1940 declaring publicly: 'America is determined not to be embroiled in the war and she is determined that neither her ships nor her nationals shall be the cause of embroiling her.'[7] This was for public consumption and simply echoed Roosevelt's own overtly neutral statements at a time when the isolationist groups including the Irish-Americans were in the ascendant. Privately, Gray had optimistic hopes that rapprochement between the north and the south would bring Ireland into the war on the side of Britain, or at least give her the ports. On his way to Ireland, Gray had visited Pope Pius XII at Roosevelt's suggestion but 'found His Holiness distinctly non-committal on the thorny Irish question' (would anyone blame him?)[8]

In May 1940 when Germany overran the Low Countries and invaded France, de Valera asked Gray if 'the United States Government could proclaim the Irish status quo vital to American interests' in view of Ireland's strategic position commanding Atlantic air and sea traffic. Gray passed on the request which Roosevelt, on the advice of his Secretary of State, Cordell Hull, rejected saying such a declaration would be a departure from America's traditional policies concerning Europe and would only lead to confusion in Europe and the United States.[9]

In June, with fears growing of a German invasion or a British pre-emptive occupation, de Valera made a formal request to the USA for aircraft, armoured cars and rifles which Gray supported and at de Valera's suggestion he travelled to Belfast to meet Craigavon, but with the negative results already recorded. Gray continued to support Irish requests for American military equipment throughout the summer of 1940 but he put his foot down when Dublin asked for a single destroyer, cabling: 'The Irish Government has no more use for one destroyer than I have for a white elephant.' A consignment of 20,000

American rifles eventually got to Ireland thanks to combined efforts by Gray, Maffey and Brennan, the Irish minister in Washington.

By the following November with Roosevelt safely re-elected with the help of the traditional Irish Democratic vote, Gray grew less tolerant of Irish neutrality. He began to campaign vigorously for the handover of the Irish ports, not just in private talks with Walshe at External Affairs but at social functions in the American legation in the Phoenix Park where he cultivated a collection of Ascendancy, pro-British and Fine Gael elements much to the irritation of the government. Gray's own disillusionment with de Valera at this time is shown in a despatch to Washington:

> His whole power is based on his genius for engendering and utilising anti-British sentiment. His administration otherwise is generally unsuccessful. He is probably the most adroit politician in Europe and he honestly believes that all he does is for the good of his country. He has the qualities of martyr, fanatic and Machiavelli. No one can outwit, frighten or blandish him. Remember that he is not pro-German, nor personally anti-British, but only pro-de Valera.

In an interview with de Valera soon afterwards in which Gray urged the handing over of the ports, the latter took a tough line saying that 'Americans could be cruel if their interests were affected and Ireland should expect little or no sympathy if the British took the ports'.[10] De Valera could have now no illusions about Gray's attitude towards him or his policy of neutrality so it is surprising to find that when Gray deliberately set a trap by hinting that a special emissary be sent from Ireland to the United States to buy arms, ships and supplies, de Valera should have fallen for it.

On 24 February 1941 Maffey telegraphed to London that the Irish government proposed to send the Minister for the Co-ordination of Defensive Measures, Frank Aiken, and a diplomatist, Sean Nunan, to the United States to get supplies, arms and ships, and that they had asked for the help of the British government to secure a speedy passage via Lisbon. Maffey added: 'Aiken is anti-British but certainly not pro-German. He is not impressive and rather stupid. I hope that every assistance will be given. It will help dispel the idea that our economic measures are punitive. Furthermore, personal contact with outside opinion will do immense good here where views are narrow and insular.' Maffey continued:

G

Idea originated in a suggestion by U.S. Minister here who hinted that a useful purpose would be served by despatch of envoy from here. He tells me that in his view main purpose served would be educational. He does not think any of Mission's objectives will be achieved. From our point of view he considers Aiken a most satisfactory choice and his advice is that we should facilitate journey in every way possible. He is strongly recommending the plan to his own Government.[11]

Nothing loth, Whitehall immediately arranged for Aiken and Nunan to fly from London to Lisbon and there connect with the Pan-American clipper service to the United States but there was a mix-up and Aiken had to spend nine days waiting in Lisbon. Maffey took advantage of the delay (one wonders how fortuitous it was) to brief the British ambassador in Washington, Lord Halifax, on how to handle Aiken when he got there, 'as it is important that he should return in chastened mood'. Maffey was especially anxious lest Aiken had been authorised by de Valera to propose some formula whereby the Irish government would ask for British help in the case of a German invasion and thereby secure the release of American arms beforehand. Gray had been urging such a formula on de Valera, apparently unaware of the extent of co-operation between the army staffs north and south.

The Foreign Office was getting worried on another count. On 12 March, while Aiken was kicking his heels in Lisbon, the US minister in London, Hershel Johnson, informed Sir Alexander Cadogan, head of the Foreign Office, that the Irish government had already been told concerning the Aiken mission that the only practical means of obtaining arms in the USA would be through the British Purchasing Commission there. The Foreign Office cabled the British consulate in New York where the BPC operated: 'This suggests that U.S. authorities may intend to try and throw on us the onus of refusing supplies to Eire. This we should naturally wish to avoid and hope you will do your best to prevent it happening.' The British reluctance to take the United States fully into her confidence regarding her dealings with Ireland was to continue to be a significant feature in Anglo-American relations for the rest of the war.

Aiken finally arrived in New York on 18 March and an interview was arranged with the president for 7 April. But five days earlier Cadogan at the Foreign Office had cabled Lord Halifax in Washington: 'Immediate, Secret. Further information has now been received from most secret sources indicating Aiken is not only anti-British but also hopes for and believes in German victory.'[12] This dubious piece of information contradicted Maffey's assessment of Aiken recorded earlier and did not come from Maffey's office in Dublin as the file shows a copy of Cadogan's telegram was passed on to the Dominions Office. The author's view is that the pro-German accusation was fed to Gray by one of Aiken's political opponents in Dublin and that Gray passed it on to London. Whatever its origin it meant trouble for Aiken as Halifax managed to get in to see Roosevelt just a few hours before Aiken was due. Halifax reported Roosevelt as saying that he did not see how Aiken could get military supplies in the United States which was certainly not going to supply any ships to transport them nor did he imagine the British would either. On the margin of Halifax's report, V. Cavendish-Bentinck, head of the Dominions Intelligence Department of the Foreign Office, noted: 'The U.S. President and Government seem to be dealing with Mr Aiken as we desire. No further action seems required.'

The Foreign Office had good reason to sit back and admire their expert sabotage operation – Aiken's interview with Roosevelt was predictably disastrous and Bob Brennan, who was with Aiken, gives a graphic account of it.[13] Roosevelt came out fighting and accused Aiken of saying that 'the Irish had nothing to fear from a German victory'. Aiken denied it and asked for proof but Roosevelt ignored such details and continued to harangue him at such length that when the president's aide, Colonel Watson, appeared discreetly at the door of the office – the prearranged signal for the end of the interview – Aiken had scarcely got a word in. He courageously ignored Watson and tried to pin Roosevelt down on supplies for Ireland. Watson then had the idea of sending in a Negro servant to start arranging the delph and cutlery on the president's desk for his lunch. Aiken pressed on doggedly and when Roosevelt offered to supply aircraft for submarine-spotting patrols off the Irish coast, Aiken blundered badly and said Ireland was not bothered by submarines but feared an attempt at an invasion and he assumed that Ireland would have the president's sympathy in the case of aggression.

'Yes,' said Roosevelt, 'German aggression.'

'Or British aggression,' said Aiken.

Roosevelt flew into a temper and said it was 'preposterous' to suggest that Britain had any intention of becoming an aggressor in the case of Ireland. 'If that is so,' cut in Aiken, 'why cannot they say so. We have asked them to . . .'

'What you have to fear is German aggression,' thundered Roosevelt.

'Or British aggression,' Aiken repeated stubbornly.

At this Roosevelt lost his temper altogether and pulled the table-cloth and all the silver off his desk roaring 'Preposterous'. The flying silver and crockery was certainly a more effective signal that the interview was over than Colonel Watson's cough but Aiken, unabashed, again asked for a guarantee from Britain that she would not invade Ireland. At this point Brennan intervened diplomatically, perhaps saving Roosevelt from an apoplectic fit which might have changed the history of the world, and he suggested that Roosevelt might point out to Churchill that if he gave such a guarantee it could ease the situation considerably. Roosevelt snapped that he would get the guarantee in the morning. He did not but it is interesting that five weeks later on 13 May, Eden reported that in a talk with the American ambassador, John G. Winant, the latter said he hoped that in the event of the British government contemplating any action aimed at taking over the ports, they would let the American Government know before such action was taken. Cranborne replied to Eden's memo saying: 'As you know, we are not contemplating any such violent action at the present time. If we do we will certainly let Washington know; but I do not anticipate our forcibly taking over the ports.'[14]

Meanwhile, back in Dublin Gray was beginning to get uneasy about his scheme for educating Frank Aiken to the hard facts of Roosevelt's foreign policy and the day after the stormy interview between the two men he cabled Washington: 'The Irish Government is exploiting Aiken's mission as American approval of its policy, at the same time making political capital out of inciting anti-British sentiment . . . I believe that the time has come for a firmer attitude and the demand that de Valera clarify definitely his position.'

Gray also suggested that he be authorised to protest against the statement made by de Valera in his St Patrick's Day broadcast to America that the belligerents 'in blockading each other are blockading us'. Hull agreed. Gray at the same time did the Irish government an immense service by arranging for a credit of $14 million for the purchase in

America of a Panamanian ship of 8,000 tons to load for Ireland a cargo of paint, soap, metal, confectionery and peas.

On 11 April, Aiken called on Hull and began by expounding on Britain's bad treatment of Ireland down the centuries, 'all of which,' commented Hull, 'I thought related very little to the realities of the present situation'. Hull then launched into an hour-long lecture of American foreign policy since 1933 boring Aiken stiff and prompting him to remark to Brennan on the way out: 'The poor old man. Why have they left him so long in that post?' Instead of coming home duly 'chastened', Aiken then took off on a six-week tour of the USA, visiting all the major cities and addressing Irish-American groups on Ireland's determination to remain neutral and the economic difficulties involved. He took the precaution of lodging a version of his speech with the State Department and adhering to this version wherever he went to forestall any further efforts to smear him as pro-Nazi. It was a wise precaution as the Foreign Office files show that British consuls and informants around the USA faithfully reported Aiken's meetings.

There was a suspicion in London, and even in certain circles in Dublin, that the Irish-American groups, who were to some extent sponsoring Aiken's country-wide tour and who were lobbying against American entry into the war out of hostility to Britain, were being financed by German gold. Barely a month before Aiken went to the USA, the German Foreign Minister, Ribbentrop, asked the German embassy and New York consulate for reports on opinion in Irish circles about England's plans for Ireland as well as the position of the Irish government and people in the event of military action by England such as the seizure of the ports. Ribbentrop's telegram continued: 'Because of the importance of all reliable information on this question for our conduct of the war, I request that you cultivate as much as possible relations with the leading Irish there so that you may be able to obtain information from them continuously. The money to be spent for this purpose will be placed at your disposal at once upon request.'[15]

In response to Ribbentrop's request for information about the use being made of Irish groups, the German chargé d'affaires in Washington, Herr Thomsen, listed his activities in this field:

I have made it a particular point, through the Special Attaché for Press Affairs in the Embassy, to cultivate relations with the Irish-American press and Irish-American leaders and their organisations. I am also personally in touch with the well-known champion of the Irish freedom movement in Congress, Senator Murray of Montana . . . By spending considerable sums from the War Press Fund, we make use of the Irish-American newspaper, *The New York Enquirer*, whose circulation we have in various ways greatly increased. Moreover, the *Enquirer* arranges for us cooperation with other Irish newspapers, such as the *Gaelic American* and *The Leader*, which is published in California. Also, through Consul-General Kapp, we maintain relations with Father Coughlin [the 'radio priest' and organiser of the populist Union for Social Justice] and his newspaper, *Social Justice*.

It would have been surprising if the American security services did not have a shrewd idea of the German efforts to manipulate the Irish pressure groups. Their sponsorship of Aiken in America through the umbrella organisation the Friends of Irish Neutrality would have aroused suspicion that the Irish minister was also being used, unwittingly or not, to serve German diplomatic aims.

Aiken's coast-to-coast performances in America were not endearing him in any case to the pro-British State Department and pressure was being put on Brennan, according to a British diplomat's report, 'to arrange for the return of General Aiken as he is becoming a great nuisance over here'. Gray was to underline the official hostility to Aiken even more clearly when he met de Valera on 28 April to read him two memoranda. The first was a protest against the 'double blockade' speech and Gray reported that de Valera 'flushed angrily and shouted that it was impertinent to question the statements of a Head of State'. He pointed out that the statement had been first made the previous January and there had been no protest then, and he went on to explain how Ireland was being squeezed economically by recent British measures.

The second memorandum was an offer by the United States government to negotiate the transfer of two freighters to Ireland for transporting food, but Gray was instructed to make the offer direct to de Valera and to say that it had been observed with regret in Washington that Aiken's 'attitude towards the British appeared to be that of blind hostility'. De Valera was in a quandary as the ships were badly needed but he was reluctant to let Aiken down. He refused the ships and loyally defended Aiken who, he said, agreed with him that a German victory would be a calamity for Ireland. Several weeks later President Roosevelt announced at a Press conference that he was offering two ships to Ireland and $500,000 from the Red Cross to purchase food

supplies but no arms were to be sold. Aiken was with Colonel Lindbergh soon after this and the latter recorded in his journal that Aiken
commented: 'I'd hate like hell to think our nuisance value was only
half a million dollars.'

The Roosevelt offer took de Valera by surprise and was at first an
embarrassment as naturally he had not publicised his earlier refusal of the
ships. Now that the offer was public he could hardly say that he was
refusing it to save Aiken's feelings. In Dublin the *Irish Press* gave the
Reuter account of Roosevelt's offer and noted that there was no
immediate government reaction. It tacked on a few paragraphs that
Aiken had been in the United States for several weeks to get food and
defence supplies and let the readers draw their own conclusions.

After the shambles of the Aiken visit it is not surprising that hostility
to Gray in Dublin reached a new pitch. Brennan in Washington urged
that de Valera demand Gray's recall as he blamed him for some of the
wilder reports in American newspapers about alleged German espionage in Ireland. On 15 May 1941, Maffey reported to London that de
Valera 'appears to be starting a campaign against Mr Gray'. He had
gone out of his way to tell some visitors that Gray was little less than a
disaster as a representative of his country and was doing great harm in
Dublin. These visitors, including Senator McGillicuddy of the Reeks,
had hot-footed it around to Maffey to tell him. Maffey suggested that
in view of Gray's valuable help to 'our cause', London could put in a
good word for Gray in Washington through Halifax. Maffey said that
it was not easy for an American in Ireland to be critical of the Irish
and their leaders and Gray was genuinely fond of the country and the
people, 'in fact he started with alarming prejudices but he very soon
and very rapidly lost sympathy with its present leadership and trend'.
It was ironic that a week later de Valera was to feel deeply grateful to
Gray for his help in averting the threat of conscription in Northern
Ireland which could have given the demoralised IRA a new lease of
life.

In March 1941, the GOC Northern Ireland had inquired about
additional home defence battalions and this had led to a discussion in the
War Office about the possibility of conscription providing the extra
troops, but then it was realised that the 5th Division with a corps headquarters was on its way to Northern Ireland and this would eliminate
the need of conscription. But the Stormont Government had got wind

of it and pushed conscription very hard with Churchill who was sympathetic to the idea as were some members of the war cabinet who pointed to the bad feeling caused by strapping young men from Northern Ireland doing civilian work in Britain and being billeted in homes where older men had been called up. This was the second time the conscription threat had arisen as Northern Ireland had been included in the provisions of the compulsory training Act in May 1939, and de Valera had cancelled a visit to the United States to have treatment for his eyes and to visit the World Fair to campaign successfully against its extension to the north.

Churchill was quite determined this time to push conscription for Northern Ireland and half the Stormont Government were over at Chequers on 24 May for the drafting of the Bill. However, two days later Churchill yielded to a formidable campaign advising against the move supported by, among others, the American ambassador in London, the Canadian Prime Minister, Mackenzie King, the Inspector General of the Royal Ulster Constabulary, Mr Wickham, the Catholic Primate of All Ireland, Cardinal McRory, whose see was in Armagh in Northern Ireland, and of course de Valera himself who twice sent Dulanty to see Churchill. On this occasion Churchill dismissed de Valera's protest, but he was unwilling to risk offending the United States. Mackenzie King pointed out that he and his colleagues 'would be grateful if possible repercussions which such a step might have upon public opinion in Canada might also be considered . . . the more it is possible to avoid the conscription issue becoming a matter of acute controversy, the less difficult, I feel sure, will be the task of maintaining Canadian unity'.[16] Even the Northern Ireland Prime Minister, J. M. Andrews, conceded finally that 'the strength of the opposition would be more widespread than had been realised' and the real test was whether conscription 'would be for the good of the Empire'. The Stormont Government had been embarrassed at the comparatively low rate of voluntary enlistment with only 38,000 volunteers out of an eligible male population of 212,000 and they probably hoped that conscription would cover up this apparent lack of enthusiasm among loyalists to fight for the embattled Empire. Estimates of the number of volunteers from Eire in the services were so high at one stage immediately after the war that the Stormont Government protested that it made their contribution look embarrassingly small. The most likely

So much for Loyalty

figure for Eire volunteers in the British forces seems to be 60,000 of whom 40,000 crossed the border to enlist in Belfast and the remainder joined up in Britain, but this last contingent cannot be accurately measured as they would have had British addresses.[17] It is clear that the figure sometimes quoted of 150,000 Eire volunteers is grossly inflated, but 100,000 Irishmen and women working in munitions factories is a reasonable enough estimate. Emigration from the south to Britain between 1940 and 1944 was approximately 160,000 and would have been higher if a limited ban had not been placed on the emigration of certain categories in 1944 on the pretext that essential services would be endangered.

On the night of 30 May, Dublin was bombed by the Germans leaving thirty-four dead, ninety injured and 300 houses destroyed or damaged. A few weeks later the German government expressed regrets about the bombing which 'may have been due to high wind' and promised to pay compensation. It was the West German Federal Government which eventually paid £327,000 ($1·3 million) in compensation in 1958. In his memoirs, Churchill theorised that the bombing of Dublin could have been an unforeseen result of British interference with the radio beams used by the German bombers to home in on their targets, but no proof has since appeared from German records that this was so.

The previous month, on the night of 15–16 April, the first really heavy air-raid on an Irish city had taken place when Belfast suffered 700 killed and more than 1,000 injured. When de Valera was woken up at home to be told the news he at once ordered fire-engines from Dublin, Dun Laoghaire, Dundalk and Drogheda to rush to the stricken city. This neighbourly gesture was deeply appreciated in the north and the Belfast newspapers and the Minister of Public Security, Mr J. C. McDermott expressed their gratitude. Curiously enough, de Valera waited several days before he made a public reference to the bombing and expressed his sympathy. Strictly speaking he had committed a breach of neutrality in sending the fire-engines across the border, so to follow this action by a condemnation of the bombing could have provoked a German riposte. Belfast had a second heavy raid on 4–5 May when even more bombs were dropped than on the previous attack, but this time the shipyards were the target and the death toll of 150 was much less.

A different Dublin preoccupation with the north emerged later that summer when there were reports of American technicians building a new naval base at Derry, apparently as part of the USA commitment to defend Iceland. When de Valera instructed Brennan in Washington to ascertain American intentions and point out that Northern Ireland was regarded as 'part of the national territory', Brennan in his own words was given 'the brush-off' and told the matter should be taken up with the Government of the United Kingdom of Great Britain and Northern Ireland.

Notes to this chapter are on pp 181–2

Chapter 7

'Now Is Your Chance'

———◆———

At 1.30am on Monday, 8 December 1941, de Valera was aroused from his sleep at his house in Blackrock, Co Dublin, by the telephone ringing. It was Walshe of External Affairs to say that Maffey had a message from Churchill which he had been instructed to hand to de Valera immediately. The urgency of this early morning call seemed ominous to de Valera as the day before the Japanese had attacked Pearl Harbor, an action which was finally to bring the USA into the war, and the message from Churchill could well be an ultimatum to Ireland to follow suit. Deeply perturbed, de Valera telephoned the Chief of Staff, Lt-General McKenna, and the Secretary to the Government, Maurice Moynihan, to stand by.

Soon afterwards, Maffey arrived and handed de Valera the message: FOLLOWING FROM MR CHURCHILL FOR MR DE VALERA. PERSONAL. PRIVATE AND SECRET. BEGINS. NOW IS YOUR CHANCE. NOW OR NEVER. 'A NATION ONCE AGAIN'. AM VERY READY TO MEET YOU AT ANY TIME. ENDS.

At least it was not an ultimatum, but de Valera was naturally taken aback at the elliptical language and its implications. He told Maffey that he thought it was Churchill's way of intimating 'now is the chance for taking action which would ultimately lead to the unification of the country' but he did not see it that way. There was no opportunity at the moment to secure unity, and the people were determined on their attitude of neutrality. Consequently, he was not in favour of going over to meet Churchill as the likely disagreement might leave conditions worse than before. He was also afraid that such a visit would be misunderstood by the Irish people and given a significance which it would not really have. Maffey replied that he understood de Valera's position but he urged him not to turn down the proposition immediately.[1] Two days later the war cabinet was told that de Valera had invited the Dominions Secretary, Lord Cranborne, to Dublin 'with as little publicity as possible'.

Cranborne met de Valera in Dublin on the morning of 17 December for what he described as 'a long, friendly, but fruitless talk'.[2] De Valera began immediately on partition pointing out that until it was settled there was no chance of Ireland abandoning neutrality, and if he tried to lead the country into the war 'his influence would be gone and the country would be split from top to bottom'. Cranborne said this was a counsel of despair for if Eire remained neutral until the end of the war, neither the British people nor the people of the six counties would consider any form of unification of the two territories, involving the handing over of the northern ports (Derry and Belfast) which had proved essential to their survival, to a government which had failed to stand by their side in the present emergency.

De Valera replied that he recognised that some postponement of the solution of partition might be inevitable, but he did not rule out the possibility that after the war different counsels would prevail. He then repeated the counter-proposal he had put to Malcolm MacDonald in June 1940 that while remaining neutral, a unified federal-style Ireland could enter into a joint strategic plan for the defence of the British Isles. Cranborne dismissed this and said 'the only chance of bringing nearer a unification of Ireland lay in the North and South of Ireland fighting together in the present war and thus creating a community of interest'. And so the conversation went on in the vicious circle pattern with which Maffey had become familiar. Cranborne ended his report thus: 'He [de Valera] said that he, too, had now come to the conclusion that we should win the war. His difficulty in rallying to the Allied cause came not from lack of sympathy, but because, he said, in existing circumstances, with the Partition problem an open sore any attempt to bring a United Ireland into the war at our side would be doomed to failure. From this position, I could not budge him.'

It was clear from the conversation that Churchill's impulsive gesture had not meant, as de Valera had at first believed, a fresh offer of Irish unity in exchange for the abandonment of neutrality. From the beginning of the war, Irish-American opinion and influence had been a restraining factor in British policy towards Ireland, but it had been often said in London that the eventual entry of the USA into the war would remove this prop for Irish neutrality and Churchill's 'now or never' clarion call was meant to be the final push rather than an invitation to work out a package deal.

In fact, de Valera had already made it clear publicly two days before he met Cranborne that Pearl Harbor would make no difference. In a speech in Cork he expressed sympathy for the American people and spoke of the traditional links, but was adamant there would be no change in policy and that Ireland could only be a 'friendly neutral'. Any other policy would have divided the Irish people and 'for a divided people to fling itself into this war would be to commit suicide'.

One would have imagined that the American minister, David Gray, would have been deeply disappointed at this further example of what he would regard as de Valera's obstinacy, but if he was he did not show it to Cranborne who had taken advantage of his visit to Dublin to meet Gray. Indeed Cranborne was somewhat dismayed to find that Gray was advocating a policy of supplying arms to Ireland because he now felt there could be no danger of an Irish government taking hostile action against both Britain and the USA. Cranborne, however, did not share Gray's enthusiasm for a well-publicised gift of allied war material to Ireland, and he pointed out that public opinion in Britain would be hostile. The fact that Britain was already supplying arms to Ireland was carefully kept from the British public who would have found it hard to square such a policy with the 'official' view as purveyed through Fleet Street that Eire was a treacherous neutral who frolicked with Axis diplomats and allowed pro-Nazi IRA men to run around freely.

Gray's proposal to supply arms to the Irish defence forces angered Churchill when he was informed of it while having talks with his new ally, President Roosevelt, on a warship in mid-Atlantic. In a waspish note to Cranborne, Churchill said he hoped there was no question of giving additional arms to southern Ireland or of asking the USA to do so at that juncture. American-Irish pressure would grow and the arrival of American forces in Northern Ireland would create a powerful impression. He ended: 'We must give full play to the powerful forces working on our behalf and not weaken their actions by minor and premature concessions.'[3]

But Churchill had left a flank uncovered, and the Irish slipped in cleverly to exploit the growing divergence of views between the allies on how to handle Irish neutrality. The Foreign Secretary, Eden, had a somewhat embarrassing interview with the US ambassador, John G. Winant, when the latter produced a telegram from Washington stating that Dublin was claiming to have been receiving military supplies from Britain and citing a speech by de Valera on 5 January that they were getting 'more and more arms'.

Churchill read Eden's report of the meeting and with growing anger minuted: 'Foreign Secretary. No arms for de Valera till he comes in (except for a few trifles by R.A.F. in return for conveniences). We request most incessantly that *no arms be supplied by U.S.* This would spoil the whole market. If necessary I will telegraph President personally.'

Irritation in Whitehall with Gray's intrusion into their carefully laid plans for dealing with de Valera grew when Maffey sent over a report on a scheme for leasing the bases to the USA which Gray had passed on to Washington. An unnamed group of Irish people friendly to Britain and the United States had proposed to Gray that the American government should appeal to the Irish government for help to win the battle of the Atlantic while offering: (*a*) to arm Eire fully; (*b*) to contribute to food supplies and industrial needs; (*c*) to pay cash for bases; (*d*) to guarantee return of same; (*e*) to use good offices to end partition; and (*f*) to consider other proposals. The group urged that these proposals be put secretly by the USA to the Irish government but with the right reserved to publish them if rejected and so force de Valera to have them discussed publicly and in the Dail. The group believed that de Valera would be overruled then or the country would be divided leaving him only the support of an extremist minority. Gray advised Washington to continue the present policy but that if a change became inevitable then the Irish group's proposals might be the best procedure.

Cranborne commented sourly that Winant's inquisitiveness about British arms supplies to Eire was probably inspired by Gray's action and he continued:

> This does not appear to be one of Mr Gray's most helpful efforts. Why put these rather woolly ideas into the minds of his Government at the present juncture? The situation is developing quite satisfactorily – Mr de Valera's most unwise reaction to the arrival of American troops in Northern

Ireland can have done him no good either in the U.S. or Eire itself. The great thing now both for HMG and the American Government is to sit tight and let him make a few more mistakes. Then the situation may be ripe for another step. But to raise the issue of Partition now would merely raise de Valera's hopes and stiffen his attitude.

American pressure continued on Eden for a full disclosure of what arms Britain was supplying to the Irish defence forces and in an interview with Winant on 20 February, Eden admitted that at the end of November a small quantity of material was released to the Irish army. This comprised: twelve anti-aircraft guns for the defence of the aerodromes at Baldonnel, Collinstown and Rineanna; four 18-pounders with ammunition; twelve 7·5mm guns and ammunition; and in January, two 6in naval guns for the defence of the mouth of the Shannon. What Eden did not disclose, but a Foreign Office official had written it into the file, was the doubly embarrassing fact that it was Churchill himself who had ordered the release of this material 'to promote good feeling between the Eire Army and British troops in Northern Ireland'.

It is a tribute to de Valera's tremendous influence in Ireland that the entry of the United States into the war was not accompanied by a nation-wide reappraisal of his neutrality policy. The strict censorship system would have been a serious obstacle for any pressure group seeking a change of policy such as the one which approached Gray, but not an insuperable obstacle. The only real resistance in political terms to the continuance of neutrality after America's entry came predictably from James Dillon, the deputy leader of the Fine Gael party. The previous July he had created a sensation in Ireland and abroad when he urged: 'We should ascertain precisely what cooperation Great Britain and the United States of America may require to ensure success against the Nazi attempt at world conquest and, as expeditiously as possible, to afford to the United States of America and Great Britain that cooperation to the limit of our resources.' He ruled out the sending of Irish troops abroad but said that this help should include 'naval and air bases'.[4] As a fervent Catholic, Dillon based his plea for aid to the allies (although America was not yet in the war) on moral and spiritual grounds, and he was virtually the sole voice in the Dail to denounce the fundamental evil of the Nazi philosophy. He also frequently criticised Aiken for his rigorous censorship of any reports of persecution of the churches in Germany and the occupied countries. For his solitary and courageous stand, Dillon was reviled by some Fianna Fáil deputies, disowned by his party leader, Mr Cosgrave, and another colleague, General Mulcahy, while de Valera himself said Dillon's speech should be censored and he totally dismissed the 'Christian crusade' argument. De Valera's irritation was increased when the foreign Press wrongly put great significance on the speech because they assumed that as deputy leader of Fine Gael, Dillon was an influential figure. In fact he was totally isolated in the Dail, and in the Senate his views were supported by only one or two men such as Frank MacDermot.

Naturally enough, Dillon was closely cultivated by Maffey and Gray and the former was reporting to London six months before Dillon's speech that it was to be expected at a suitable moment. With the entry of the United States into the war, Dillon made a last but vain effort to bring his party with him on the question of giving active aid to the allies when at the annual Fine Gael conference on 10 February 1942 he declared with a typical rhetorical flourish: 'Whatever the sacrifice, whatever America may want from us to protect her from her enemies, she will get it for the asking.' Ten days later he resigned from Fine Gael and became an Independent deputy in the Dail. He rejoined the party some years after the war. Gray reported that Dillon's speech had not been well received even by pro-American elements in Ireland and that it was badly timed.[5]

When the first American troops landed in Northern Ireland on 26 January 1942 as Operation Magnet (part of the overall Plan Bolero which was to bring 1¼ million US troops into the United Kingdom in 1942), de Valera complained that his government had not been consulted and reasserted the claim 'for the union of the whole national territory and for supreme jurisdiction over it'. When Brennan in Washington handed over the text of de Valera's statement to Sumner Welles he added orally, and obviously under instructions, 'that the Irish Government and people regarded the landing of American troops in Northern Ireland as an official sanction by the United States of the Partition of Ireland and increasingly believed that these troops were going to be used to attack Irish forces'.[6] Brennan agreed with Welles that this belief was 'fantastic and incredible' but maintained that it existed in Ireland.

Roosevelt was taken aback at the sinister motives being attributed to

Operation Magnet, but having learned something of Irish ticklishness from Mr Aiken the year before, he kept his temper and assured de Valera in a personal message that there was not, and 'is not now, the slightest thought or intention of invading Irish territory or threatening Irish security'. This was the sort of guarantee that de Valera had sought in vain from Churchill, and he was highly pleased at Roosevelt's response. He decided to push his luck further and in a letter to Roosevelt in April thanked him for the assurances but repeated his objections to the American troops in the north on the basis of partition and asked for military supplies. Roosevelt in a memo to Sumner Welles commented exasperatedly: 'If he would only come out of the clouds and quit talking about the quarter of a million Irishmen ready to fight if they had the weapons, we would all have higher regard for him. Personally I do not believe that there are more than one thousand trained soldiers in the whole of the Free State. Even they are probably efficient only in the use of rifles and shotguns.'

Roosevelt would have had to retract his sarcastic remarks if he could have witnessed the manoeuvres, or 'mimic war' as the Irish Press quaintly termed them, held near the south coast the following September. At this stage the permanent defence forces totalled just under 40,000 and this included about 30,000 'durationists' or men who joined up for as long as the emergency lasted. In addition there was a part-time Local Defence Force of 98,000 men who would have been immediately incorporated into the regular army if hostilities broke out. There was also a part-time Local Security Force of older men which carried out auxiliary police duties, traffic control, ARP work and first-aid and this force numbered about 100,000.

The 1942 manoeuvres were the biggest ever held in the country, and simulated a battle between a Red and Blue army across the River Blackwater in south Munster with the 1st and 2nd Divisions as the opposing armies. The aim of the manoeuvres was to test the ability of the defence forces to hold an invading force from crossing the river for as long as was practical. The ordinary soldiers were not, of course, told that the invader was presumed to be German and that the help they would be holding out for was the British army in the north. The latter trained for the W plan in manoeuvres held in an east-west direction across Northern Ireland, while senior liaison officers from the south observed in mufti or British uniform. British liaison officers who came

H

south posed as ARP advisers and wore appropriate badges.[7] Hempel and his staff were not fooled by such devices, but they probably helped to avoid awkward questions being asked.

Keeping morale high in the defence forces was not an easy task especially from 1943 on when the threat of invasion visibly receded. However, there was a theory held in the highest quarters, and by de Valera himself, that the reverses being suffered by the Germans on the eastern front could prompt the High Command to risk a do-or-die strike at England through Ireland. In February 1943, Maffey reported a talk with de Valera in which he urged the need for arming Eire against a possible German coup, but Maffey said that if such an attempt were made Britain would be able to deal with it satisfactorily from the air.[8] The combination of low pay and frustration led to a fairly high rate of desertions from the Irish army and after the war the Minister for Defence, Mr Traynor, gave the figure as 7,000 out of the 40,000 who were in the regular army for the duration. Just over 4,000 deserters crossed the border to enlist in the British forces according to the minister who denied the estimate of 12,000 given in the Catholic newspaper *The Tablet*.

Two main recruiting drives were launched, the first in June 1940, the second in November 1941, but the government were never fully satisfied with the results and veiled threats of conscription were occasionally made. The appeal of the army was perhaps unwisely pitched at too materialistic a level. One typical poster read:

THE ARMY WANTS MEN
YOU WILL LIKE LIFE IN THE ARMY

As well as training you the Army will look after your health and comfort. There are Physical Training Instructors to build up your muscle and bone, to say nothing of three good hot meals a day, a bed in warm, comfortable quarters and enough pay to keep you in cigarettes and other things you like. There are books to read, concerts got up specially for your benefit and hurling, boxing and other athletics to keep you fit. Besides these there are doctors and dentists in case you are in need of them. WHAT MORE DO YOU WANT? You will have the satisfaction of knowing you are doing the right thing at the right time. And that counts too.

The 'what more do you want' approach was an insult to the thousands of young men who did not volunteer for hot meals and a

warm bed but simply to defend their country with inadequate equipment against an invader who might be German or who might be
English. This uncertainty also contributed to a rather schizophrenic
feeling in the army with the men in the 1st Division in the south men-
tally anticipating a German landing, and those in the 2nd Division in
the northern part of the country facing towards the border with the
possibility of having to oppose a British invasion. A well-kept secret
during the war was that the GOC of the 2nd Division, Maj-General
Hugo McNeill, at one stage approached Hempel to sound him out
about possible German help against a British invasion. This only became known after the war when German records were captured but it
shows the strain imposed on men with the responsibility of defending
their country with hopelessly inadequate equipment.

The Irish navy and air force were known officially as the Marine
Service and the Air Corps, and although an effort was made to build
them up during the wartime period they remained pathetically small.
When the war broke out there was no navy at all and the two ancient
fisheries protection vessels, the *Muirchu* and the *Fort Rannock* were
commissioned on 15 January 1940 as Public Armed Ships. A week
earlier the first motor torpedo boat, built by Thornycrofts in Britain,
had been handed over to the Marine Service and over the next two
years the number was increased to six. The MTBs were more of a
morale booster than anything else as they were unsuitable for patrolling
except in fairly calm weather. A naval reserve called the Maritime
Inscription and consisting of keen amateurs such as fishermen and
yachtsmen, was also set up and helped to enforce the port control
system around the coast. There was also a coast-watching service
whose lookout posts were on virtually every headland and linked by
telephone with command headquarters.

The Air Corps was somewhat better equipped than the Marine
Service. There was a squadron of Hurricanes (some of which had been
repaired after crash landings by RAF pilots who were interned) and
another squadron of Hawker Hectors. Just before the war the Air
Corps had taken delivery of less than a dozen Lysanders of an advanced
design which permitted take-off and landing in limited space. There
was also an under-strength squadron of Avro Anson medium bombers,
a few Avro trainers, three amphibious Walruses based at Rineanna
(now Shannon Airport) which did coastal patrolling, and three

Gloucester Gladiators nicknamed as their more famous counterparts in
Malta, 'Faith', 'Hope' and 'Charity'. The main base was Baldonnel
aerodrome south-west of Dublin guarded by some light anti-aircraft
batteries which on one memorable Saturday nearly shot down in error
the 'Honeymoon Special' which came up from Rineanna every weekend with pilots on leave. The army staff had virtually no idea how to
make use of this small but keen air force if hostilities did break out, and
the former commanding officer Colonel Patrick Swan recalls with disgust that once when a German invasion was believed to be imminent,
he and the other pilots were ordered into slit trenches with rifles to
pick off descending paratroopers while their precious aircraft were left
exposed helplessly on the runways as obstructions.[9]

In Britain there was a campaign led by the Irish-born General
Gough, who had commanded the Fifth Army in World War I, for the
revival of the historic Irish regiments from Munster and Leinster where
all the southern Irishmen in the British army could serve. Churchill
liked the idea commenting: 'We have Free French and Vichy French
so why not Loyal Irish and Dublin Irish.' He also wanted a 'Shamrock
Wing' formed in the RAF. The War Office was definitely not enthusiastic as they saw a danger that de Valera would regard such all-
Irish units as a breach of neutrality and that he would ban the enlistment of Irish men in the British forces.[10] A compromise was reached
at the end of 1941 when an Irish Brigade was discreetly formed and
inserted into the 1st Division. The brigade consisted of one battalion
each from the Royal Irish Fusiliers, the Royal Inniskilling Fusiliers
and the Royal Ulster Rifles. In fact, only half of the brigade was Irish
and it was decided that no publicity would be given to it until it had
distinguished itself in action.[11]

The RAF's Shamrock Wing never got off the ground, and in fact
the RAF was far more interested in getting back the forty-six pilots
and aircrew who were interned in Eire from late 1940 onwards as
they crash-landed or baled out. They and their 260 German counterparts (including 160 sailors rescued in December 1943) were interned
in special quarters in the Curragh military camp. Life was fairly
pleasant with parole freely granted for visiting friends, going to dances
and following university courses.[12] Subsistence pay was provided by
their respective diplomatic missions which also passed on any com-
plaints they had to the Department of External Affairs. The British felt

the restraints on their liberty all the more keenly as freedom was only sixty miles away across the border. The first British internee, Lieutenant Mayhew, was ordered by the War Office not to accept parole but this order was soon changed. Fraternisation between British and Germans outside the camp was not unknown in some cases, but the British protested at Germans being allowed to attend the same dances.

There were three major escape attempts by the British internees and of the twenty-two involved, eleven got away to fight again with the help of Irish sympathisers, and a well-known Dublin doctor was given a suspended prison sentence and a heavy fine for his role in the escapes. The camp commandant, Colonel T. McNally, complained bitterly to headquarters after one escape claiming that the British internees concerned had broken their parole and should be sent back from the north. Only one German internee, Conrad Neymeyer, escaped and he succeeded in getting aboard an Irish ship bound for Lisbon, but was captured by the British authorities when the ship called at Cardiff for the usual controls.[13]

For three years Maffey negotiated with de Valera and Walshe for the release of the British internees, and he finally got agreement with help from Gray that only pilots and crew on 'operational flights' should be interned while those who crashed on training flights could be allowed to return home. In October 1943, twenty-one British airmen were released discreetly and driven in cars across the border. The German internees were informed that the British were being moved to a new camp at Gormanstown and one of them, who now lives in Ireland, believes that still. The operational flight rule was a major concession by de Valera to Britain and it was liberally interpreted although eight British internees were not released until June 1944. American airmen who landed in the south were never interned as they were always on 'training flights', but their landings and infringements of Irish air space became so frequent and embarrassing after the arrival of the Americans in the north that the word EIRE was printed in letters about thirty feet high with white stones on about sixty headlands around the coast. General Hill who commanded the American air force in Northern Ireland then flew around the coast in a Fying Fortress with General McKenna noting every sign and its identifying number and this information proved to be an invaluable navigational aid for the inexperienced American pilots. The figures for crashes were: 39 American aircraft with 15 killed; 16 German aircraft with 26 killed and 105 British with 182 killed.

As 1942 passed by with no sign of the American entry into the war having any substantial effect on Irish neutrality, Maffey and Gray began to look ahead to the general election due in 1943 as a possible way of removing the stubborn de Valera from the scene and replacing him with a more co-operative government. There was indeed a possibility that Fianna Fáil's eighteen-vote overall majority would be wiped out in the election as there was widespread discontent in the country at social conditions. The high unemployment, emigration and shortages were due to factors outside the government's control but it was blamed all the same. Industrial discontent was further increased by the wages standstill order introduced under emergency powers in 1941 which also outlawed strikes for higher wages. But while wages were frozen or increased very little, the cost of living bounded up because of shortages, and between 1939 and 1946 the cost of living index rose by two-thirds but the average industrial wage by only one-third. The government also introduced an unpopular Trade Union Bill which split the trade union movement and aroused much bitterness. The compulsory tillage campaign had antagonised much of the rural community.

On the afternoon of Sunday, 28 October, Maffey visited the leader of the Fine Gael opposition party, Mr W. T. Cosgrave, father of the present leader of the party who became Taoiseach in March 1973. Maffey sounded him out cautiously on the election, which Cosgrave expected to be held in January 1943, as he had heard that the government had asked the Catholic hierarchy for its consent to a Sunday election but was refused. Cosgrave said he expected Fianna Fáil to lose about thirty seats and Labour to gain about twenty, with Fine Gael staying constant and the Independents showing a small increase.

In his report of the conversation, Maffey said that in these conditions a national government of the three main parties was the most likely with Cosgrave as the leader since Fine Gael and Labour would out-number Fianna Fáil.[14] Even if Labour refused to join such a coalition and de Valera headed a Fianna Fáil-Fine Gael alliance, Maffey thought such a government would have a more generous regard for British interests, especially if Frank Aiken were ousted. Cosgrave told Maffey forcefully that it would be quite hopeless for any government to attempt to change the policy of neutrality as its hold in the nation's mind seemed to him 'to strengthen rather than to diminish'. But Maffey was hopeful that Fine Gael would be able to tilt the balance more in the allied interest and cited a conversation with a prominent front-bench member of the party, Dr O'Higgins, who had pointed out to him that a feature of Fine Gael which 'may operate in Britain's favour was their regard for Mr Churchill whose part in the Treaty negotiations of 1921 is not forgotten by their leaders today'.

Maffey had sensed from his conversation with Cosgrave that in spite of the growing strength of the neutrality policy, it could still possibly be undermined by American pressure including that of Irish-Americans. Maffey had impressed Attlee at the Dominions Office with this view and in February 1943 the latter wrote to Eden, the Foreign Secretary, suggesting that the British ambassador in Washington, Lord Halifax, could be asked for his views on preparing American opinion, especially Irish-Americans, for an approach for bases in Ireland after the election.[15]

Eden was willing enough and wrote to Halifax on the lines suggested, but added that he was doubtful if they could really hope for much American help in this matter and he warned Halifax not to say anything to the United States authorities at this stage 'which might lead them to believe that we were even contemplating an approach to them on this issue.'

David Gray, however, decided to force the pace and, unaware that for the past two years Britain had been deliberately applying an economic squeeze to try and wring concessions on bases from de Valera, he sat down on 26 February 1943 and drafted a plan to do precisely the same thing. This draft was in the form of a letter to the Chargé d'Affaires at the US embassy in London, H. Freeman Matthews. It was a curious move on Gray's part. He told Matthews that he was contemplating a despatch to the State Department on the lines of his letter but he did not want 'to start anything' which could embarrass Winant, the ambassador in London and therefore Matthews's immediate superior, without first canvassing British opinion.

In his letter, Gray referred to several Anglo-Irish trade deals which were being arranged whereby Britain supplied raw materials such as rubber and leather for Irish industries to process and export back to Britain while keeping a fixed amount for Irish use. Gray showed his disapproval and also referred with distaste to the news of another wheat-beer deal; he heartily approved, however, of the banning of the

arrangement whereby Irish farmers would grow vegetables for the
American troops in Northern Ireland. He went on:

> It is growing clearer with the passing months that only by awakening the
> Irish people to the realities of their isolationism and making neutrality
> cease to be economically advantageous can any change be brought about in
> Irish public opinion . . . a punitive policy is not suggested, but only the
> cessation of continuing benefits for which no acknowledgement is made
> or any common advantage conceded. The British departmental chiefs may
> naturally feel that Eire is their special sphere of influence in economic
> matters but the fact remains that the so-called 'Irish problem' remains the
> most important and dangerous single obstacle to Anglo-American under-
> standing and cooperation and if this opportunity for settling it by
> educating the Irish nation to the realities of their position is neglected, the
> consequences are likely to be far-reaching and disastrous.

Gray was taking Maffey fully into his confidence and had given him
a copy of his letter to Matthews which Maffey sent to London where
Eden found it 'interesting and realistic' but Attlee, still in charge of the
Dominions Office, was more reserved. In fact Attlee was getting uneasy
at the way Maffey and Gray were now influencing each other. In a
letter to Eden on the Dominions Office position on 5 March 1943,
Attlee said that Maffey had been in London a few days previously and
had suggested that if Britain thought that occupation of the Irish bases
was really important, they might consider asking Roosevelt to ask de
Valera for them on behalf of the United Nations and that if the request
was put in that way de Valera would find it difficult to refuse it out-
right. De Valera could also be told that the request and his reply
would be made public.

Attlee had told Maffey that he was not in favour of this line at the
present time as there had been no demand from the staffs for strategic
facilities in Eire for some time and he doubted whether they were now
'of very great importance'. Neither was it clear that Roosevelt would
be willing to act as 'cat's paw' for Britain in this. If de Valera said no
as he expected, strong feelings would be aroused in Britain and the
United States which could lead to action to their disadvantage. If de
Valera said yes it would be tantamount to bringing Eire into the war
and Britain would have to undertake to provide her with not only
military protection such as anti-aircraft equipment but also with
civilian supplies. He observed: 'I thought it very doubtful whether we

could spare enough of this at the present time and that the strategic facilities would probably be very dearly bought at such a price.'[16]

This was surely one of the most revealing comments during the whole wartime period on British and American efforts to bring Ireland into the war. If in 1943 Britain felt unable to give Ireland the necessary supplies and protection against German air-raids when the Reich was already beginning to stagger, what would have been the position in 1940 and 1941 when in a few nights the German air force could have devastated southern Ireland's mere half-dozen towns and cities with populations over 20,000? Neither Maffey nor Gray seem to have had much sympathy for this aspect of Irish neutrality. Their view as diplomats was constricted in a way in which that of politicians such as Attlee, Roosevelt and even Churchill was not. The latter three, in spite of their irritation with de Valera, could understand something of his reluctance to take the step which would expose his people to the horrors of modern warfare; Maffey and Gray increasingly saw de Valera as the sole obstacle to the success of their mission. They conveniently forgot the popular support for neutrality and as time passed this personal dislike of de Valera affected their judgement, but to a much greater degree in the case of Gray.

On 12 May Halifax was advised that Gray was on his way to Washington and that he might not be carrying on much longer. A word of appreciation to Roosevelt or Hull 'might not only give pleasure but do something to ensure that Gray's eventual successor is someone not less friendly and helpful'.

Gray was not ready for retirement yet and he had plenty of ideas for making things hot for neutral Ireland. Halifax had a meeting with him and reported back to London on 18 June. Gray had made the following points: (*a*) the North African landings the previous December had a 'tremendous effect on Irish opinion' concerning the allies' prospects of winning the war; (*b*) if the allies ever wanted to take over the Irish ports it would not cause very much trouble but Gray thought that if it was ever done, it should be by US sea forces rather than by Britain or from Northern Ireland; (*c*) Gray was apprehensive about the appeals he foresaw de Valera making later to American opinion in favour of Eire being allowed to sit in at peace talks and in favour of putting pressure on Britain in the matter of partition. His remedy for this was that the United States should pick a quarrel on grounds of their own choosing, presumably the ports issue, before that time arrived. The effect of this would be, in Gray's view, that American opinion would be less sympathetic to pleas from Eire, especially if, as he felt sure, de Valera lost his temper in the process.

Thus was the scene being set for that curious melodrama which was played out in February and March 1944 in Dublin, Washington, London and the Dominion capitals and is still referred to in Ireland laconically as the American note.

Notes to this chapter are on p 182

Chapter 8

Setting the Trap

The seeds for the so-called American note were planted in Gray's brain six months before in February 1943 when Maffey and the Canadian High Commissioner in Dublin, John Kearney, told him that they had been discussing what action could be taken to improve the position of the British Commonwealth and if possible of the United Nations as regards Eire.[1] Maffey and Kearney felt that a properly planned move could result either in practical benefits for the allied war effort or, if these were not forthcoming, in a clarification of Eire's position in the post-war period which the Dublin government should be invited to state without undue delay.

It was suggested, therefore, that a request be made for 'the ports'. If granted, the allies would have much needed facilities and if not, Eire would be definitely on record as having refused a specific request made now for the first time. Otherwise she might say with truth, 'You never asked us for the ports.' It was feared that if the record was not made clear, 'Eire would be in a better position later on to claim benefits to which she was not entitled on the basis of her attitude during the war.' What especially worried the allied diplomats in Dublin was how the Irish government would be able to cash in on the large numbers of Irish volunteers in the British forces to claim post-war advantages.

Maffey and Kearney proposed to Gray that the United States 'should act as spokesman' in the plan for joint action and Gray enthusiastically agreed. But as we have seen in the previous chapter, Maffey got no encouragement in London for a new approach to de Valera on the

ports, Attlee had pointed out that there was no pressure from the
military staffs for these facilities and that Anglo-Irish relations were as
satisfactory as could be expected. Kearney had received a similar response from Ottawa. Maffey and Kearney who had primed Gray for a
fresh initiative against de Valera, had now been brought to heel by their
respective masters but once launched, Gray was not going to be so
easily put off.

By May 1943, it was clear that the Irish elections were only a matter
of weeks away and Gray could no longer restrain himself so he sent
Washington a 5,000-word memorandum ponderously entitled
'Memorandum by the Minister in Ireland on Recommendations for
the Adoption of a Joint Anglo-American Economic Policy Towards
Eire Shaped With Reference to Political Considerations.' Gray tried
to show that the Irish dependence on British goodwill for economic
survival had, instead of producing appropriate feelings of gratitude for
continued British supplies and a shift away from strict neutrality, only
made the Irish more deeply ensconced in a world of unreality. The
main point he tried to bring home to Washington was the threat to
Anglo-Irish relations from de Valera's claim to *de jure* sovereignty over
Northern Ireland 'which it is now apparent that he plans to use to the
end of creating post-war disagreement between Britain and the United
States, if not to foment trouble in Northern Ireland to the detriment of
the common war effort'.

Gray urged that action was needed which would convey a 'sobering
warning' to de Valera and provide 'an educational experience' for the
Irish people as to their essential dependence on the United Nations. He
proposed four courses:

(1) A demand in the name of the United Nations for the lease of air and
port facilities etc.

(2) A demand that Axis Missions be removed, on the ground that their
presence is a menace to United Nations' vital interests.

(3) A demand that Eire clarify her position towards the British Commonwealth of Nations. Is she in or out?

An unsatisfactory reply to any of these demands would result in the
progressive shutting off of raw materials for Irish industries, on the
ground that if Eire chose to exercise her right to an isolationist position,
she must assume responsibility for her own supply.

(4) Perhaps the most effective manner of meeting the issue from the

American political viewpoint would be the enforcement of conscription in Northern Ireland . . .

This last proposal from Gray reveals his confused thinking on Irish affairs. Exactly two years previously while the USA was still neutral he strongly advised against Britain imposing conscription in the north unless there was at least an escape clause for Catholics. But now in 1943, according to Gray, American opinion would be glad to see Northern Ireland 'slackers' called up and although bloodshed seemed unavoidable 'it could, however, be truthfully said that new bloodshed could hardly increase the political capital manufactured out of the executions of 1916'. Mr Gray was reaching the stage where he was becoming unable to distinguish adequately between Irish nationalist rhetoric and the cautious realism which underlay it, and trouble was brewing as a result.

The election on 22 June was a setback for de Valera as his party, Fianna Fáil, lost the absolute majority which it had enjoyed since 1938, but for the main opposition party, Fine Gael, the result was disastrous with a loss of thirteen seats. The small Labour party, on the other hand, won the highest representation in its history with seventeen seats. The 1943 election also saw sizeable support for the new farmers' party Clann na Talmhain and its decision not to oppose the re-nomination of de Valera as Taoiseach allowed the Fianna Fáil Government to continue in office. The campaign had been a lively one with Fine Gael on the defensive as a result of the unfair Fianna Fáil innuendoes that they alone were the true guardians of neutrality. One slick election slogan was: 'If you vote Fianna Fáil, the bombs won't fall.' Government speakers, rattled by the vigorous campaigns by the *Irish Independent* and the *Irish Times* for a national coalition government, warned that 'foreign people' would represent a defeat for the government as a rejection of the neutrality policy, thus ignoring the fact that neutrality had been supported by all parties since the war had begun.

Gray's long memorandum had been read by Roosevelt who, only a few weeks before, had told Eden on a visit to the United States that his policy towards Eire was to ignore her completely. He was now beginning to have different thoughts and he asked Hull for his views on the Gray paper. Hull warned the president:

The Irish and the British have fought one another for seven hundred years. They suspect and distrust one another. Each tries on suitable occasions to obtain the support of the American people and Government against the other. We must be careful, therefore to be sure that any action which we take in this regard has a sound military basis in the opinion of our own Chiefs of Staff. It seems to me that this is of fundamental importance to make it impossible for anyone to maintain that we took sides with the British against the Irish and 'pulled British chestnuts out of the fire.'[2]

When the Joint Chiefs of Staff reported to Roosevelt on 11 August 1943 on the military aspects of acquiring air and naval bases in Ireland, it was to the effect that they did not see any necessity for them in the forseeable future even if they did mean more flexibility for air transport and air ferry operations. The report made it clear that the Chiefs of Staff did not want to be obliged to take over bases in Ireland. But Roosevelt had not waited for this report before making up his mind, as two days earlier Halifax was reporting to London that the president was now considering a formal approach to de Valera to ask for the lease of ports in the south and west of Ireland and possible air bases as well on the grounds of saving American lives. Halifax added that Roosevelt thought de Valera would disagree but it would 'make the record right and it would be useful to have it recorded that he had refused'.

Having got Roosevelt's semi-approval for an approach to de Valera on the ports, Gray moved fast and he had a draft letter ready by August 1943 which Roosevelt gave to Churchill when the latter visited him at Hyde Park.[3] Gray's draft letter was a shortened version of his long-winded memorandum of the previous May. It recalled in some detail various examples of American forbearance and aid to Ireland during the past three years.

Referring to de Valera's pledge of a policy of 'benevolent neutrality' towards the United States given during his speech in Cork soon after Pearl Harbor, Gray claimed that because of Ireland's geographical position her neutrality had operated in favour of the Axis powers. Another factor which 'still further weighs down the balance of Irish neutrality in favour of our enemies', the draft Roosevelt letter continued, was the presence in Eire of diplomatic representatives of Germany, Italy and Japan as they were in a favourable position to spy on the allies while the allied diplomats in Dublin were not in a favourable position to spy on the Axis powers. The espionage danger was further increased by 'the number of misguided but reputable Irish nationals' who opposed the Irish government and looked to the Axis powers as the hope of Irish liberty.

It was naïve also to believe, the draft letter went on, that the Nazi régime which had prepared and precipitated the downfall of Austria, Czechoslovakia, Poland, Norway, Belgium, Holland, France, Greece and Yugoslavia by fifth column organisation had not also laid the groundwork for 'an inside job on Eire'. Such a conclusion was supported by 'the recrudescence and mysterious financing of the banned IRA in 1938, the capture of parachutists and sea-borne agents in Eire possessing large sums of money and the strange escape from prison and long-time harbouring of a convicted German spy by respected Irish citizens'. This last reference was to Sergeant Gunther Schuetz whom the Abwehr parachuted into Ireland in March 1941 equipped with the new microdot code system, but he was arrested within hours by suspicious policemen as he wandered along a quiet country road in Co Wexford with a heavy suitcase. He claimed he was a South African called Hans Marschener but the Irish intelligence officers had already picked up his principal contact, a long-established German businessman in Dublin called Werner Unland, and later even cracked the microdot code. With the help of IRA members Schuetz, dressed as a woman, managed a daring escape from Mountjoy Jail in March 1942 and had been sheltered by the Brugha family for about a month before being re-captured. Mrs Brugha was the widow of Cathal Brugha who had played a leading role in the Anglo-Irish struggle as a colleague of de Valera and had been the first noted republican to be killed in the civil war which followed. A street in Dublin is called after him. At the time of the Schuetz episode his widow was running one of Ireland's best-known shirt companies. The respect for the Brugha name in Fianna Fáil did not prevent the government interning a son and daughter of the family for IRA activities. By the time Gray was trying to build up his case that Ireland was an important centre for Axis espionage, both Goertz and Schuetz – the two Abwehr agents who had been at liberty the longest – had been transferred with their handful of colleagues to military custody in Athlone barracks. But Gray's point was valid enough none the less. German agents with the right contacts could be hidden and supported for longish periods by respectable Irish families for whom England was still the 'ancient enemy'.

After the lengthy preliminary statement, the Roosevelt letter as drafted by Gray came to the point. Now that the outcome of the war was no longer in doubt it appeared to the American government to be a friendly act 'to offer the Irish people a share in that victory' as it had given them a share in their supplies. How could this be done? Simple enough: 'While it is true that regardless of your decision we shall win the war, it is also true that Eire can play a notable and honourable part in contributing to the shortening of its duration by leasing us bases for the protection of the Atlantic supply lines and by the elimination of Axis spy centres on Eire territory.' The real threat was in the tail: 'The American Government trusts that your Excellency will favour them with a reply at your early convenience and will understand that the American Government's obligation to the American people will require the publication of this note and your reply thereto.'

As soon as Churchill returned with this draft of Roosevelt's proposed letter to de Valera from his meeting with the president at his home at Hyde Park, he circulated it among the war cabinet for their views and it figured on the agenda for 3 and 29 September. Unfortunately, three memoranda which the cabinet discussed concerning the Roosevelt letter at the second meeting have not been released for inspection at the Public Record Office, possibly to spare Mr de Valera embarrassment. The American ambassador, John G. Winant, reported from London that the war cabinet was divided over the Roosevelt letter. The following November Maffey told Gray that some ministers in the cabinet were so anti-de Valera that they did not want him to be even given the chance of coming into the war on the allied side at that stage by agreeing to lease bases and recall the Axis diplomats.

Another intriguing element was the rift that began to open up between Gray and Hull over the draft Roosevelt letter. No sooner had Gray got in with his version than Hull began drafting his own which he described as 'preferable' to Gray's. In an exchange of correspondence, Gray defended his version and criticised the 'mildness' of Hull's draft which was now submitted to Eden for British approval. But the British had become increasingly wary of any direct American approach to de Valera on the ports and their stalling irritated Hull and the State Department where Stettinius, who had replaced Sumner Welles as Under Secretary, surmised on 28 October that the British might be trying to kill the American approach by inaction. Gray was also getting

Page 133 (above) *Mr de Valera inspects troops on a route march passing through a Co Kildare village. A large part of training consisted of long-distance marching and for the manoeuvres of August–September 1942, the men of the 2nd Division based in the northern half of the country marched to Cork and after three weeks of intensive exercises marched back to base while being 'attacked' by units of the Local Defence Force; (below) men of the Maritime Inscription, or naval reserve, parade down O'Connell Street, Dublin. Note the ugly air-raid shelters in the middle of the street between the statues. Colonel Anthony Lawlor, who inspired the idea of the country's first volunteer naval reserve, borrowed the title from the similar force set up in seventeenth-century France by Louis XIV's minister, Colbert.*

"How ya, Frank?"

Page 134
(left) *This is how Mr Frank Aiken's American visit was portrayed on the cover of Dublin Opinion in April 1941. His official reception was cooler than Lady Liberty's however; (below) Mr James Dillon after casting his vote in the 1943 general election in Co Monaghan. He was re-elected easily although he was the only member of the Dail or Lower House to advocate that Ireland give the allies the use of the Atlantic ports and any other facilities they needed.*

more impatient and when the Portuguese government created a sensation by agreeing to lease bases in the Azores to its 'oldest ally', Britain,
Gray urged that this was the best 'psychological moment' to follow up
with the request for Irish bases.

It was not until 17 December 1943, that Eden wrote to Winant asking
the US government 'to postpone for the present' the approach to de
Valera they had in mind.[4] Eden pointed out that the British government had twice tried to bring Eire into the war, the first time by means
of the Malcolm MacDonald mission in June 1940 and the second time
when Cranborne went to Dublin in December 1941 just after Pearl
Harbor and Churchill's 'now is your chance' midnight appeal. On
both occasions, Eden wrote, de Valera made it clear that until the
question of partition was settled there was no chance of Eire abandoning
her neutrality and he gave no undertaking that this would happen even
then. Eden continued: 'Any reopening of the issue of Partition in this
form at the present time would, however, be extremely embarrassing
to the United Kingdom Government, in view of the very strong views
which are widely held on this question, both in Great Britain and
Northern Ireland.'

One would have thought that there the matter ended, but the indefatigable Gray was already at work drafting yet another note. This
time he left out any mention of the ports or bases and only requested
the recall of the Axis diplomats. He was to have better luck with this
effort as we shall see in the next chapter.

While Gray was preparing his surprise for the unsuspecting Irish,
some interesting developments had taken place on the war scene which
had their effect in Dublin. In July of 1943 the allies had invaded Sicily
and within three weeks Mussolini had resigned and been replaced by
Badoglio. The Italian minister in Dublin, Berardis, who had harassed
Italian café owners in the poorer areas of the city to wear black shirts
and display pictures of Mussolini on national holidays, now changed
allegiance without any bother after he had tearfully requested Irish
government help to draft an announcement of the changed circumstances in Rome. Berardis now joined in the campaign to have his recent
ally, Hempel, recalled to Berlin. Apparently, he had never liked or
trusted Hempel, especially since May 1940 when the Irish security
forces in a round-up arrested Liam Walsh, an Irishman working in the
Italian legation, who was suspected of working secretly for a German

I

propaganda organisation, the Fichtebund. Although it was unlikely that Hempel knew of this, the Department of External Affairs did not enlighten Berardis who concluded that the arrested man had been deliberately planted by the German legation to know what was going on in Berardis's mission.

The bombing of Rome by American planes during July which resulted in over a hundred deaths and about a thousand casualties and caused some damage to the Church of San Lorenzo just inside the Vatican area, brought effusive messages of sympathy for the Pope from de Valera and the Archbishop of Dublin, Dr McQuaid, at the damage done to 'the sacred monuments' but no word of sympathy for the human victims.

This governmental and episcopal preoccupation with the fate of 'sacred monuments' at a stage in the war when millions of women, children and old people had been slaughtered by order of the Third Reich contrasts oddly with the absence of public protest in the south at the savage bombing of Belfast or the persecution of Catholics and Jews in countries under Nazi domination. Mr Aiken's censorship duly suppressed reports of atrocities coming from underground sources in the occupied countries, but there was a good idea of what was going on under Nazi rule even if the full horror of the concentration camps was yet to be revealed. One can understand something of Gray's irritation with a system of censorship which allowed full publicity for Cardinal McRory's attack on British and American troops in the north for 'overrunning our country' yet suppressed the reference to the 'accursed bombers' in a pastoral letter by a bishop whose diocese had suffered several fatalities from German bombs.

Traces of anti-semitism lurked beneath the surface of Irish life and made ugly appearances from time to time. The constitution of 1937 officially 'recognised' the Jewish congregations in Ireland as well as the Church of Ireland (Anglican), the Presbyterian Church, the Methodist Church, and Society of Friends. This recognition by the state was certainly welcome to the Jews in Ireland at a time when the Nazi persecution was already under way, but it has recently been revealed that the government refused a request from the Vatican just before the war began to give temporary refuge to a certain number of Jewish doctors.[5]

The appeal was refused by the then Minister for Justice, Mr

Ruttledge, on the grounds that the Medical Registration Council would object strongly to the admission of foreign members of the medical profession while a large number of Irish citizens who qualified as doctors every year were forced to emigrate. That there was more than just an economic issue involved seems clear from a despatch from the Papal Nuncio to the Vatican saying that the committee which was trying to organise the affair was very discouraged by the amount of anti-Jewish feeling that had been encountered. A refugees' committee did, however, facilitate at this time the settling in Ireland of Jewish intellectuals who got posts in the universities and later in the Institute of Advanced Studies.

A court case in January 1942 in which a landlady successfully defended her right to refuse a tenancy to a Jewish dentist, throws an interesting light on the position of Jews in Ireland at that time. The judgement was given by one of the most eminent Irish judges, Mr Justice Gavan Duffy. He said: 'The question is whether Mrs Schlegel had unreasonably refused her consent. Like her husband she was Irish and a Catholic. On ascertaining that Mr Gros was a Jew, she refused consent explaining: "Their principles are not ours; they are anti-Christian and I could not have an anti-Christian living in the house where I live." '

The judge went on to say that he found that Mrs Schlegel's objection represented a genuine and deep-rooted feeling. It had been characterised as 'a caprice and as mere prejudice'. Caprice was not the right word for anti-semitism, which far from being a particular crochet, was 'notoriously shared by a number of other citizens'.

The 1943 election brought to the Dail a young deputy called Oliver Flanagan whose head was stuffed with half-digested monetary theories and 'Jewish conspiracy' theories which were propagated by an otherwise saintly priest called Father Fahy. Soon after his election, Flanagan made an outburst in the Dail:

How is it that we do not see any of these Acts [Emergency Orders] directed against the Jews who crucified Our Saviour 1900 years ago and who are crucifying us every day of the week? How is it that we do not see them directed against the Masonic Order? How is it that the IRA is considered an illegal organisation while the Masonic Order is not considered an illegal organisation? There is one thing that Germany did and that was to rout the Jews out of their country. Until we rout the Jews out of this country it does not matter a hair's breadth what Orders you make.[6]

It is sad that Flanagan's intervention was left unanswered. Some months later, Mr McGilligan, a former Minister for External Affairs, told the Minister for Justice, Mr Boland, that there was a suspicion that Jews were 'more favoured' than others when sentences were being remitted. Socially there was a certain amount of ostracism of Jews in golf clubs and bridge clubs but it was fairly muted. The silence of the Catholic hierarchy on the Nazi persecution of the Jews was deafening and contrasted with the indictments by the American bishops and Cardinal Hinsley in England which were published in the Irish newspapers. Perhaps the censorship was an inhibiting factor, but one suspects there was never much interest by the Irish bishops in the fate of what the Good Friday liturgy termed the 'perfidious Jews'.

Notes to this chapter are on p 180

Chapter 9

The American Note

On two nights in late December 1943 German bombers flew over Co Clare on Ireland's west coast but instead of bombs plummeting down on unsuspecting rural homesteads getting ready for yet another wartime Christmas, two parachutists floated down gently from the wintry sky. The first arrival on 16 December was a local man called John O'Reilly, well known as the son of an ex-policeman who lived in Kilkee, but he was arrested within hours and whisked off to internment in Arbour Hill military prison in Dublin. A similar fate awaited the second parachutist, John Kenny, who landed in Clare three nights later.

O'Reilly, who had landed with a radio set and a set of codes, had been half expected by the Irish security authorities since he had stopped broadcasting for the German Rundfunk's Irish section about six months previously. He had been one of the several dozen Irishmen working in hotels and at fruitpicking in the Channel Islands when they were occupied by the Germans in summer 1940, and like a number of his compatriots O'Reilly had volunteered to go to Germany and engage in propaganda work. For O'Reilly this meant regular broadcasts on the Irish section of the German radio, and he used the pseudonym Pat O'Brien.

The Germans tried hard to win Irish support through their powerful radio services. As far back as December 1939 the Hamburg and Bremen stations began regular broadcasts in Gaelic by Dr Ludwig Muhlhausen, Professor of Celtic Studies in Berlin University. He was well known in Irish university circles and broadcast in fluent Gaelic using the Kerry dialect. Lord Haw-Haw, or William Joyce from Co Galway, was of course the best-known Irish voice on German radio during the war, and Irish listeners enjoyed his sarcastic sallies such as his remark that the Irish army 'could not beat the tinkers out of Galway'.

The Irish authorities could feel pleased with their smart work in picking up so quickly the latest German 'spies' (more likely only interested in the free trip home to Ireland), but the incident held serious implications which they would only realise two months later. The arrival of Messrs O'Reilly and Kenny by courtesy of the Luftwaffe had in fact coincided with the latest effort of the American minister, David Gray, to indict de Valera and his neutrality policy as morally contemptible and, from a security point of view, as a serious danger to the allied war effort now preparing for the opening of the second front in Western Europe.

In the last chapter we saw that the British government had politely rejected the proposed American approach to de Valera requesting the use of bases if it became necessary because of the likelihood that de Valera would reopen the partition issue, with consequent embarrassment all around. But Gray now thought he had hit on a way to put de Valera on the spot without running this risk and he drafted a note which made no mention of bases but requested the withdrawal of the Axis missions in Dublin on the grounds of the security risk they involved for the allies getting ready for D-Day.[1]

This time the British were ready to back Gray. Cranborne recommended to the war cabinet that they agree to the proposed American approach to Eire and that the best way for the British government to participate would be to send a separate note to the effect that they had been consulted by the American government and warmly approved their initiative. On the question of whether the approach should be made public, Cranborne advised that it should be a matter for further consultation.[2]

In a reply to Cranborne on 2 February, Churchill showed great anxiety about the possibilities of the Axis missions in Dublin damaging the success of Overlord (the codeword for the impending allied landings in Normandy) and said it might be necessary, if they remained at their posts, 'to sever all contacts between Ireland and the Continent in the near future for a period of months'. But even if complete severance was imposed 'it would not prevent the German Ambassador from sending a wireless warning of Zero even though that was the last he was able to send'.³ In fact several weeks beforehand Hempel had finally yielded to Irish pressure and had handed over the contentious radio set which he had been told to stop using for sending weather reports back in September 1941. At that time the USA was not yet in the war and for his diplomatic telegrams Hempel was cabling to Washington where the German embassy radioed them to Berlin. After Pearl Harbor Hempel could no longer use this channel, and the Irish authorities who were monitoring all his radio messages (although it seems doubtful if they ever broke his code) insisted that the radio be stopped. There is still some suspicion in Dublin that Hempel supplied a stream of weather reports to assist the escape through the Channel from Brest of the German warships *Gneisenau, Scharnhorst* and *Prinz Eugen* in February 1942. After that time the legation radio seems to have been effectively silenced, but it was not until the end of 1943 that Hempel could be persuaded to hand it over to a Dublin bank for joint custody. But no more than Churchill could de Valera be absolutely sure that Hempel, or one of his staff, did not still have the means to flash one vital radio signal which could help to wreck Overlord, and on 21 February at 3.30pm Gray stood in de Valera's office with the note which could yet seal this potential security leak.

The note was a condensed version of the long-winded memoranda which he had been pouring out for the State Department's benefit since the previous March, recording American generosity and forbearance towards Eire and the latter's lack of gratitude in return. This latest note concentrated on the security risk to American shipping and forces caused by the Axis missions in Dublin and the unfair geographical advantage they had for espionage purposes. It referred to the possession of a radio set by the German minister and to the arrival two months previously of the two parachutists also with radio sets. It concluded:

> As you know from common report, United Nations military operations are in preparation in both Britain and Northern Ireland. It is vital that information from which may be deduced their nature and direction should not reach the enemy. Not only the success of the operations but the lives of thousands of United Nations soldiers are at stake. We request, therefore, that the Irish Government take appropriate steps for the recall of German and Japanese representatives in Ireland. We should be lacking in candour if

we did not state our hope that this action will take the form of severance of all diplomatic relations between Ireland and these two countries. You will, of course, readily understand the compelling reasons why we ask, *as an absolute minimum* [author's italics], the removal of these Axis representatives, whose presence in Ireland must inevitably be regarded as constituting a danger to the lives of American soldiers and to the success of Allied military operations.[4]

Gray sent Maffey a brief account of the interview with de Valera which is important in view of the reports which circulated about it at a later date.

> He [de Valera] then read the Note and at a certain point paused and said, 'Is this an ultimatum?' I replied that to the best of my knowledge and belief it was in no sense an ultimatum, nor did the text contain any 'or else' clause. He then finished the Note and said in substance, 'We have done all we could to prevent espionage directed against your interests and we can do and will do no more. As long as I am here my answer to this request must be – no.' I said that I regretted this view of our request; that it seemed to us a reasonable one and that, with due regard for the security of American lives and for the success of our military operations, we could hardly do less than make it. The Prime Minister was at all times extremely courteous. I then thanked him for having received me and took my leave.

In his report to Washington, Gray said that de Valera 'betrayed no anger as he had often done when confronted with an unacceptable proposal but looked very sour and grim'.

The following day Maffey followed Gray and presented himself before de Valera with the much shorter British note which simply said that the American request had the 'full concurrence' of the British government which fully supported the request for the removal of the Axis diplomats. But this time de Valera had a completely different reaction as Maffey's report makes only too clear:[5]

> I presented the Note to Mr. de Valera today at 4.30 p.m. After perusing it, he turned to me, white with indignation, and exlaimed, 'This is an ultimatum. This is an outrage.' I pointed out that it was none of these things and that he was taking up an unreasonable attitude to a most reasonable and justifiable request. If he were in General Eisenhower's position his anxieties would have led him to the same step. He protested hotly that everything possible had been done to save us from those anxieties. I said 'Everything except removing the root of them.' He declared that it was all part and parcel of our policy of putting a squeeze on neutrals all round the

map. He objected very much to the presentation of a Note. He and I had established a good working basis without this sort of thing. I said the formal nature of the step was necessary and fully justified by the flagrant action of the German Government in despatching official planes to Eire for espionage purposes . . . He quietened down considerably from his first passionate reaction but remained badly shaken though not in any way which indicated an attempt to understand our point of view. He professed to see nothing in the proceedings, nothing but an attempt to push him into the war and to deprive Eire of the symbols of neutrality and independence. It was obvious that he attached immense importance to this symbolic factor.

Maffey concluded his report by saying that the cabinet had been sitting all day 'no doubt concocting a reply to the American Note'. He asked for permission to tell the Canadian High Commissioner, Kearney, confidentially of the step taken, 'otherwise there is a possibility of a wedge being driven in here'. Maffey's words were prophetic as first thing the following morning, 23 February, de Valera called in Kearney before Maffey had a chance to brief him. Maffey gave London a full account of the interview:[6]

> Mr de Valera has now given a Canadian twist to the business. The Canadian Minister, knowing nothing of the Anglo-American approach, was lectured on the subject by Mr de Valera for an hour and a half yesterday morning. Fortunately, the Canadian Minister performed his part with most satisfactory candour, re-emphasising in his own way the points already made. He made it quite plain that he considered that the request was reasonable and necessary and that in his view the Axis Legations ought to be turned out. Mr de Valera, very emotional and stubborn, complained that the notes were merely a political move, that they implied a direct threat to which Eire would react, that interference with the sovereignty of Eire would be resisted, and that the army and the country would fight, and were even now preparing for eventualities. He intended to summon the Dail and receive their endorsement of this renewal of the old struggle, this time against England, against America, against anybody. The Canadian Minister, not having seen the note, naturally supposed that something in the nature of an ultimatum had been delivered. Nevertheless his reaction was admirable.

Maffey, however, was trying to put the best face on an affair which had taken an unexpected and alarming turn as far as he and Gray were concerned. It had been a serious oversight not to have kept Kearney informed and in spite of Maffey's smoothing over, he and the Canadian government were justifiably irritated. Secondly, neither Maffey nor Gray had realised the dangerous implications of the words 'absolute minimum' in the American note, and de Valera was determined to read the most threatening significance into the phrase with the hope of getting international sympathy for his opposition to an 'ultimatum' that was never meant to be one. Gray and Maffey were in trouble and they knew it.

After hearing of Maffey's stormy passage with de Valera in contrast to the 'controlled emotion' he had displayed to Gray, the latter advised, in a cable to Washington, the 'token release of strategic materials for the Sugar Company' to avoid the appearance of retaliatory action on the part of the USA. Gray predicted that de Valera would want to represent himself as a martyr and he advised: 'special pains to forestall any possible denunciation of Eire by the British Prime Minister at this time. We might lose more than we have gained by such action.'[7] Gray was right to be apprehensive of a characteristic Churchillian intervention, and his worst fears were shortly to be realised.

In his telegram Maffey let a Wagnerian mood creep in to his assessment of the situation. He saw that de Valera had deliberately decided to dramatise the situation and reported that the Defence Council had sat all night 'devising means of waging war'. Maffey felt it could hardly be possible to keep the issue on such a level, but in case of need de Valera would use the censorship ruthlessly for the purpose of staging a new martyrdom of Ireland and regaining his lost political majority in the prospect of 'a new blood sacrifice'. Maffey continued: 'He [de Valera] is a strange mixture of sincerity, hysteria and astuteness; from having led the country into a wilderness he now, as an Irish politician, sees new dynamic forces in the pent-up frustration of war years, in partition, fanned in the Catholic feelings of the moment.' This last was a reference to Cardinal McRory's Lenten Pastoral which had attracted much attention in the London Press for its assertion that in view of past ill-treatment by England, 'Eire deserves credit for not having allied herself with the Axis nations and offered them hospitality and assistance.'

London now began to get feed-back from the High Commissioner's office in Ottawa on the real Canadian reaction and not on what Maffey thought it was. Garner of the High Commission told London that

Kearney had reported from Dublin that what had infuriated de Valera was the presentation of formal notes to which he would be forced to reply by formal answer and which would then become public property. To this extent Gray's determination to get de Valera 'on the record' was working. De Valera, Kearney continued, had also taken exception to the words 'absolute minimum' which he read as a threat of invasion and he had told Kearney that Eire 'would fight invasion from any quarter and, even though the outcome was hopeless, would resist to the last man'.[8]

On 26 February, Garner told the Dominions Office that Kearney had been instructed by Ottawa to make the point that the Canadian government had had no opportunity of commenting in advance of the event and 'If they had been consulted they might have suggested the adoption of less direct and formal methods.' But the Canadian government was in full sympathy with the object of the Anglo-American approach. They would be glad to intervene if the withdrawal of the notes would make it easier for de Valera to expel the Axis diplomats, and they hoped there would be no publicity for the notes. Maffey the day before had expressed the view shared by Gray that 'publication now or in the near future leading to a press campaign would be most detrimental'. A Foreign Office official noted on the file, however, that Churchill had now written a minute saying that he hoped 'full publicity' would be accorded. The official added: 'It is however essential that the story should not break here before it breaks in the United States.'

Garner went on to say in his cable to London that there were 'certain unsatisfactory aspects' about the Canadian reply from a British point of view, but it was as favourable as could be expected. He said that Kearney was showing some irritation at not being taken earlier into confidence; that the Canadian authorities would have welcomed further explanations and a fuller account of the American note, the full text of which they were still unaware. The Canadians also felt that an informal approach would have been better and that it would have been 'helpful from the point of view of saving de Valera's face if the note could have included some "evidence" against the Axis legations'. They again stressed that they did not want any publicity and hinted that de Valera could be given a reassurance that no invasion was planned. Kearney gave de Valera this reply orally on the night of Saturday, 26

February, five days after the delivery of the American note. It was a period during which rumours had begun to circulate in Dublin and other parts of the country that an American and British invasion from the north was imminent.

On the same day as Kearney delivered orally the Canadian note which, according to Maffey, left de Valera feeling 'relieved and gratified', Brennan in Washington, on instructions from Dublin, was at the State Department expressing fears that the American note contained a threat of invasion. He was received by Hickerson of the European section who told Brennan with some sarcasm that the only sanction Eire need fear was 'the wrath of American mothers' if the Axis missions in Dublin caused the loss of their sons' lives. Hickerson confirmed categorically that the American note was not an ultimatum and said that the non-invasion pledge given by President Roosevelt in 1942 after de Valera's protest against the arrival of American troops in Northern Ireland still stood. Gray was instructed by the State Department to give de Valera these assurances personally.

The rumours which were building up to a dangerous pitch in Dublin were not altogether assuaged by de Valera's speech in Cavan on Sunday, 27 February when he said: 'At any moment the war may come upon us and we may be called to defend our rights and our freedom with our lives. Should that day come we will all face our duty with the traditional courage of our race.' This was magnificent but it was not war, and de Valera must have known that better than anyone at this stage. Both Gray and Maffey had told him there was no ultimatum, Kearney had also been reassuring, and Brennan's cable after the equally reassuring interview with Hickerson should have reached Dublin before the Cavan speech was made.

Maffey reported to London on Monday, 28 February, that, 'thousands spent the weekend convinced that an American ultimatum had been delivered, that fighting had begun on the northern border and that battleships were assembled off Howth'. Maffey and Gray tried to appear as nonchalant as possible to allay the rumours, with the former appearing at an army football game in the same box as the Minister for Defence and with Gray casually telling a cabinet minister he was going fishing for the weekend. Maffey was getting anxious and urged London that it was important that the British Press did not exaggerate the rumours. The responsibility for the rumours was clearly on the Irish side. Junior officers had gossiped about the army alert and movement of troops to the border and this idle talk had been greatly amplified in Dublin pubs. When Gray repeated to de Valera the State Department assurances given to Brennan, he pointed out that a Third Secretary in the US legation, Aaron S. Brown, had been given a substantially correct version of the American, British and Canadian notes by a person in whom de Valera had apparently confided. Gray warned de Valera that if the story broke it would not have come first from the American legation nor, did he think, from British sources.[9]

Gray was taken aback to find that de Valera was taking a grave view of Hickerson's ironic remark to Brennan that the only sanction Eire had to fear was 'the wrath of American mothers'. He professed to see a 'sinister' aspect in this becoming part of the record, and Gray tried to assure him that this was merely a 'friendly warning' of what could happen if American lives were lost. From being an affair of high drama, with de Valera being ready to fight to the last drop of Irish blood to resist an allied invasion from across the border to expel eight German and Japanese diplomats, the episode had now descended to the level of discussion about the admittedly formidable power of the American matriarchy. It was time to halt the whole business as quickly and discreetly as possible, but it was too late and the Press were on the scent. Naturally, the rumours had reached Hempel and he called on Walshe to find out what was going on. Walshe told Hempel irritably that, 'it was all due to those damned parachutists'. Later that day Walshe told Kearney that Hempel felt deeply humiliated, and Kearney asked blandly: 'Then why does he not resign?'[10]

The development that all sides feared occurred on 4 March when the *Daily Express* in London appeared with the headline, 'Eire racked by invasion scare.' The story that followed made an affair that was rapidly becoming ridiculous even more grotesque. The newspaper said that the 'official explanation' was that 'a few wild shots were fired ten days ago by a befuddled Allied soldier who crossed the border from Ulster into Eire'. Following this incident, the report continued, the Irish army was five days on the alert, forts were manned, bridges were mined, the LDF was called out, Mulcahy and O'Higgins, the chief opposition leaders, had been summoned by de Valera but refused to speak afterwards. The rumour had spread that Mulcahy had been arrested and James Dillon shot, and de Valera was said to have gone to

London. The report concluded by speculating that de Valera had been asked to make a *démarche* to Hempel 'to disprove an allegation', and that it was believed that the allies had emphasised to de Valera Eire's responsibility in preventing security leaks about the Second Front.

The Ministry of Information in London was aghast. Officials there saw the marvellous possibilities in the story for German propaganda while they were caught with their pants down and lacked any official guidance from the Foreign Office as to what was going on. The Ministry of Information immediately censored the story for the whole Press, but met angry opposition from the *Observer* who had hoped to give the story great prominence the next day. Winant, the American ambassador, had been told by the Foreign Office to have a statement ready for the Press and he had replied stiffly that he had been assured by Eden and Cranborne that there would be no publicity for the American note before there had been consultation between London and Washington. This assurance had been given by Eden, but as the Ministry of Information pointed out, all they could do when it leaked to the Press was 'hold up a story a few hours'. The ministry's mysteriously named 'man of confidence' was despatched to tour the London editors to persuade them to hold off and the Chief Press Censor, Rear Admiral G. P. Thomson, issued a directive to the Press that on security grounds nothing should appear and an explanation would follow later. When it came it said rather lamely that 'premature publicity might well prevent a satisfactory outcome of these efforts as it would give the enemy time to influence the Eire Government's decision by pressure'.

The Dominions Office was now chagrined to find that the New Zealand government sent a telegram asking 'whether at this stage the loss of goodwill through embarrassment caused to Mr de Valera and his Government would be commensurate with any particular advantage we might gain in making a major issue out of this particular matter'. The telegram also asked for evidence of Axis spying. The Dominions Office, dismayed at the lack of Commonwealth solidarity, cabled back to New Zealand that it was not possible to give 'in public' any evidence other than that of the parachutists and it denied that Britain was trying to make a major issue of the affair, saying defensively that it was an American idea inspired by military reasons.

On 7 March Brennan in Washington handed in de Valera's reply to the American note. It was a long one which began with a formal confirmation of de Valera's oral refusal to comply with the American request for the removal of the Axis missions and expressing appreciation for the assurances that the American government did not contemplate military or other measures because of the reply which had been given.

The Irish government, the reply continued, were surprised that so grave a note should have been addressed to them as its terms seemed so out of harmony with the facts and traditional relations of friendship between the Irish and American peoples. The Irish government doubted that such a note could have been presented had the American government been fully aware 'of the uniform friendly character of Irish neutrality in relation to the United States and of the measures which had been taken by the Irish Government, within the limits of their power, to safeguard American interests'. The reply went on:

> They felt, moreover, that the American Government should have realised that the removal of representatives of a foreign state on the demand of the Government to which they are accredited is universally recognized as the first step towards war, and that the Irish Government could not entertain the American proposal without a complete betrayal of their democratic trust. Irish neutrality represented the united will of the people and parliament. It is the logical consequence of Irish history and of the forced partition of national territory.

Late on the night of 10 March, Gray cabled Hull in the State Department that the Irish government were very concerned at a report on the BBC that day giving details of the American note. Gray had telephoned Winant in London and had been told that Washington had just informed him that the story had broken in London and as a result Hull was going to confirm it by publishing the American note with the comment that a negative reply had been received from the Irish government.

When Hull gave the story officially to the American Press with the text of the American and British notes, Brennan had got clearance from Dublin to have the text of the Irish reply released simultaneously. The following day, 11 March, the story of the American note made headlines around the world and stayed on the front pages for over a week thanks to an especially maladroit move by Churchill which a number concerned had only too correctly feared.

No sooner had the world Press carried the story of the exchange of notes, the fear of invasion in Eire and the measures taken by the government there to resist, than the British government announced a ban on all travel from Britain to both parts of Ireland. No official reason was given for the move, but the Press Association's diplomatic correspondent simultaneously published a story which gave the travel ban a punitive character and he hinted at the possibility of economic sanctions as well, apparently as a result of the Irish refusal to comply with the American request for the removal of the Axis missions.

The PA story was carried in all the Irish papers and Maffey was aghast. He telegraphed London the same day that this was 'a disastrous line' and he urged a ban on further Press comment on the travel restrictions. In Washington, Hull had received a report from Gray that 'all classes of Irish opinion fear economic or military sanctions by the United States and Britain' and to allay these fears Gray wanted authorisation to announce in Dublin that the American government had no intention of economic or military reprisals and was going to release previously refused supplies of steel, copper and aluminium to the Irish Sugar Company. Maffey backed this request.

Hull said he was willing to support the release of supplies for the Sugar Company but for the time being did not want to commit the USA to a pledge of no economic sanctions. While he did not think they were advisable, he felt this was primarily a question for the British government as Ireland's chief supplier. He asked Winant for any further information on the measures planned by Britain concerning Ireland, and revealed that Washington was considering a further note to de Valera reaffirming the position taken in the original approach.

Churchill himself provided the answer to Hull's request in a statement in the House of Commons on 14 March in which he said the initiative for the recent step had come from the American government with full British support. The British government had for some time past taken a number of measures to minimise the danger to the allied cause involved in the retention of the Axis missions in Dublin. Churchill continued:

> The time has now come when these measures must be strengthened, and the restrictions on travel to Ireland announced in the press yesterday are the first step in the policy designed to isolate Great Britain from Southern Ireland, and also to isolate Southern Ireland from the outer world during the critical period which is now approaching. I need scarcely say how

Page 151 (above) Like Malta, Ireland had three Gloucester Gladiators nicknamed 'Faith', 'Hope' and 'Charity' here shown flying over a part of the coastline; (below) the M1 was the first of six motor torpedo boats with which the Irish Marine and Coastwatching Service was equipped during the war years. They were not really suited for the rough seas around the Irish coast but they helped the morale of the young navy.

Page 152
(left) *Churchill's moment of triumph as he acknowledges the cheers of the crowds on VE Day in London. A week earlier in his victory speech he had made a bitter attack on Irish neutrality; (below) de Valera answers Churchill's attack in a broadcast from Dublin on the night of 17 May 1945. Cheering crowds waited for him as he left the Radio Eireann studio.*

painful it is to us to take such measures in view of the large numbers of Irishmen who are fighting so bravely in our armed forces and the many deeds of personal heroism by which they have kept alive the martial honour of the Irish race. No one, I think, can reproach us for precipitancy. No nation in the world would have been so patient . . .

Churchill's statement only added more fuel to the blaze kindled by the first announcement of travel restrictions. If Eire was to be isolated not only from Britain but also the 'outer world' how was she to survive without the coal, oil, raw materials, wheat, fertilisers and other vital supplies on which she depended to keep a semblance of normal life going? The London *Times* tried to play down the economic sanctions aspect, but Churchill's isolation threat made the following day's headlines. He had referred to Commonwealth solidarity on the approach to Ireland, and indeed statements indicating support for the request for the removal of the Axis missions from Dublin had been received from the Canadian, Australian and New Zealand governments. But this new step by Churchill raised serious anxiety in Ottawa and in a telegram to the Dominions Office the government there, while expressing relief that the travel ban was not punitive, went on to take a sharp tone:

In general it seems to us that the recent developments concerning Ireland are matters of high concern to all the members of the Commonwealth. We were not consulted in advance of the attempts to secure the removal of Axis representatives nor were we informed of your intentions respecting travel restrictions . . . If later steps are limited to actions necessary to prevent leakage of military information the Irish Government should have no reasonable cause for complaint as long as fear of ulterior political motives is not present in their minds.

This fear however undoubtedly prevails and what is done now may affect the position of Ireland in relation to the rest of the Commonwealth for many years to come. If Ireland is moved to leave the Commonwealth that is a matter of serious moment to us. We assume that no question of the expulsion of Ireland from the Commonwealth can arise except as the result of a decision reached by all the Commonwealth Governments.

In South Africa there was a long and heated parliamentary debate following the publication of the American note and the action of the leader of the Nationalist opposition party, Dr Malan, in sending a telegram of support to Mr de Valera for his stand in refusing the allied request. In the debate Malan defended his telegram saying it was not only his right but his duty to support a 'sister Dominion'. Malan said

K

that South Africa agreed with Eire's interpretation of Dominion status, namely, that Dominions had full control of their external affairs. They had the right to remain neutral even if Britain went to war and they had the right – a right they wished to exercise – to break away from the British Empire. In fact it was Malan who as nationalist prime minister (1948–59) paved the way for South Africa to leave the Commonwealth in 1961. In reply General Smuts said the day might come when they would thank God that South Africa had not followed Eire's example and stayed neutral. Had de Valera's policy of neutrality really led to national unity as the opposition claimed, asked Smuts?

Even Roosevelt was showing some unease at the line being taken by Churchill, and he sent a message to Lord Halifax to the effect that he hoped economic sanctions would not be applied to Eire. He was aware that this was a British affair but he wanted to make his views known regarding American relations with Eire and the presence of American troops in Northern Ireland. In Dublin, Gray was still extremely anxious to give a public indication that economic sanctions were not intended (it will be recalled that only nine months previously he had been urging pressure on Ireland which specifically included economic sanctions!) He had suggested to Maffey that in addition to getting the release of the supplies for the Sugar Company he would write a letter to the Press denying any intention of economic sanctions.

This attitude of Gray irritated Churchill who minuted Cranborne that it would be a great pity if Gray was to write such a letter without first consulting Britain. Churchill continued: 'We have followed the American initiative in this matter and have come forward in support. It would be very wrong for them now to explain it all away and leave us out in the open. There is no question of punishing the Irish but only of preventing the German Embassy in Dublin from betraying the movements of our Armies. This will entail isolation measures.'

Cranborne agreed heartily and minuted back to Churchill that Gray who had started the whole business 'seems now to be suffering from a bad attack of cold feet'. Cranborne went on to say that Gray's proposal to announce the release of supplies would make the American government look 'remarkably silly' and put the British government, who had loyally supported them, in a position of 'acute embarrassment'. Cranborne pointed out that further isolation measures would have to be taken and it was very important they should have American support, otherwise it would look as if Britain was taking advantage of the American note to squeeze the Irish government and 'that would be deplorable'. As a way out of this problem, Cranborne suggested to Churchill that they tell the Americans beforehand of the future isolation measures planned so as to get their public support and so defeat any attempt 'to drive a wedge between our two countries'. Cranborne also suggested that Maffey be authorised to explain privately to the government in Dublin the reasons for these measures 'so far as they can be given' so that they might be taken by agreement with Dublin and not merely imposed. Cranborne concluded: 'I do not suggest this out of any tenderness for Mr de Valera but merely because such a precedent might avoid Irish retaliation with regard to such matters as Irish labour for Britain or our security organisation in Southern Ireland which would be embarrassing for us.'

In fact Cranborne must take much responsibility for the muddle the allies had got themselves into over their notes. He knew, for example, when Gray was urging his approach to de Valera the previous January that Britain would fairly soon have to take special security measures in the form of restrictions on travel between Britain and Ireland but he did not foresee, as he should have, that the likely de Valera refusal and the British restrictions would seem to be directly linked.

In his reply to Roosevelt, on 19 March, Churchill wrote:

> Gray's lead in Ireland has been followed by us and it is too soon to begin reassuring de Valera [the first part of this sentence was omitted from the copy of this telegram reproduced in Churchill's memoirs]. A doctor telling his patient that medicine prescribed for his nerve trouble is only coloured water is senseless. To keep them guessing for a while would be much better in my opinion . . . I think that we should let fear work its healthy process rather than to allay alarm in de Valera's circles. In that way we shall get a continued stiffening up of the Irish measures behind the scenes. At the moment these are not so bad to prevent a leakage.

Churchill also advised Roosevelt that Britain did not intend to prevent anything going into Ireland or to stop the necessary trade between the two countries, but until Overlord was launched he did propose to stop ships going from Ireland to Spain, Portugal and other foreign ports. Outward-bound planes would also be stopped as well as telephone services overseas. Churchill said he would only contemplate stopping the Irish cross-channel trade if the Irish retaliated by withholding the Foynes airport facilities (used by BOAC and Pan American Airways).

The Foreign Office mandarins were clearly uneasy at the line events had taken and Greenway, who was acting head of the Dominions intelligence section, minuted: 'This will require very careful watching. President Roosevelt, having got what he wanted i.e. Mr de Valera on the record as careless of the lives of American soldiers, is now endeavouring to place his own baby firmly in our arms, and what is more, to make us pay the "paternity order".'

In Dublin, Maffey was having a series of difficult sessions with Walshe who, he reported, was deeply perturbed about Churchill's 'isolation' threat. This posed an immediate problem for the Irish government as 1,400 Irish persons with work permits were waiting to travel to Britain. If the isolation measures were going to be really drastic, the Irish government felt they would need all able-bodied men at home to cope with what could be an extremely difficult fuel and supplies situation. Walshe also offered 'all co-operation possible' to the British government to effect closer control of Axis activities in Ireland.

Maffey had become depressed at the course of events following Churchill's speech, and he reproached London for not allowing him to tell the Irish authorities more explicitly that the travel and other restrictions were for military and not punitive reasons. Hence he 'could not succeed in clearing the air of doubt and suspicion'. He sadly contrasted the apparently divergent lines of British and American policy:

> British and American Governments are now on different courses. American Note has fallen into the background. American Minister has given the Eire Government every assurance that there is no intention of following it up in any way [if this was true Gray had gone beyond Washington's instructions]. Indeed I see signs of desires to assist Eire e.g. in permitting importation of steel for Irish Sugar Co. Action in the field of restriction is to be British action.

Maffey concluded that the co-operation built up in recent years on matters such as secret intelligence, forced landings, and recruitment could probably be maintained provided he could give Dublin some assurance on Churchill's phrase and make some gesture of consulting the government on questions of mutual interest such as closing the border. De Valera had asked to see him but Maffey was holding off as he knew what de Valera would request.

At last, on 27 March, the Dominions Office gave Maffey the go-ahead to inform the Irish government of the future restrictions planned such as telephone communications, air services, and diplomatic correspondence and to ask for their co-operation stressing that the restrictions were of a military and temporary nature. He was also told to point out that because of the diversion of coastal shipping the amount of coal for weekly delivery to Ireland would be 'seriously reduced', and Mr Leydon was invited to go over to London to discuss the situation.

Maffey lost no time in going to see de Valera and clearing the air on British intentions. He reported that de Valera 'after the strain of sitting under the sword of Damocles' was greatly relieved to be informed and given a chance to co-operate in security measures.[11] He told Maffey that their old relationship had suffered but now it could be re-established. He spoke 'bitterly' of the wording of the American note and expressed doubts about the power of the Axis legations to do evil under the present restraints. Maffey strongly challenged this and said history would prove how thoroughly justified the allied request had been (as yet his prophecy has not proved correct). He continued: 'Having latterly grown somewhat doubtful as to whether the episode of the notes would after all work out to our advantage, I now feel satisfied that the instructions given me have turned the scales to our great advantage, now, and I trust, in the future.'

Walshe accompanied Leydon to London and concentrated on giving both the British and American security authorities there assurances on any necessary co-operation. His offer was accepted and a tripartite meeting between MI5, the OSS (its American counterpart) and Irish intelligence officers was arranged. This was a going-through-the-motions exercise as MI5 and G2 in Dublin had, as we have seen, been co-operating closely since the war started – in 1943 a Colonel Bruce (later a distinguished diplomat and in 1973 appointed as first US ambassador to Communist China) and a Mr 'X' of the OSS bureau in London had visited Dublin and after meeting G2 officers returned to London expressing satisfaction that the Irish authorities were taking adequate security measures. Walshe also suggested that an American security officer be based in Dublin to work closer with the Irish security authorities. This was a rather embarrassing offer for the Americans as an OSS man called Marlin, who had arrived in Dublin under the cover of being Gray's special assistant in 1942, had established a close liaison with G2 and as a former Trinity College student he knew the Irish scene well. His views and Gray's diverged more and more as the war progressed and Gray eventually asked for his transfer.

Gray apparently heard of this offer by Walshe and he sent off an extraordinary cable to Washington on 11 April which eventually fell into the hands of Lord Halifax who promptly sent it to London. In it Gray reported that 'de Valera is apparently trying to win back the allegiance of the IRA by adopting their nationalist programme . . . and he is also trying to capitalise on the help from the IRA in his underground campaign against Northern Ireland. Therefore de Valera is not going to spill inside dope to outsiders about the IRA. Cases in point are his lenient treatment of Yseult Stuart and the Brughas.' For anyone knowing the facts this was a ridiculous hotchpotch of gossip and inaccurate out-of-date material. A Foreign Office official minuted: 'I have shown this to the Dominions Office who do not attach much importance or even credence to this report.'

Gray partly redressed this piece of foolishness by co-operating with Maffey and the Foreign and Dominions Offices to dissuade Hull from going ahead with a second American note to de Valera which even Gray could see would help no one, least of all the USA. Hull reluctantly accepted this advice, and one of the factors which won him round was de Valera's action in calling a general election for 30 May. As it turned out one American note was enough to win him a handsome overall majority, but with a second one under his belt he might have felt strong enough to close down the American legation!

De Valera's election victory was a striking confirmation of the great boost to his prestige which the American note affair provided. The opposition had foolishly given de Valera the pretext for calling an election by defeating the government on a vote in the Transport Bill then going through the Dail. It was a golden opportunity for de Valera to capitalise on the strong tide of popularity then running in his favour as a result of the publicity over the American note. For the country at large it was a morale booster once the initial invasion scare had been dissipated. After almost five years of sombre neutrality, cramping censorship, high emigration and unemployment, food shortages and transport difficulties, here suddenly was Ireland back in the world's headlines and in the pose that appealed to every Irish person – standing up fearlessly to the big fellows. It did not seem to matter that the new

British restrictions were making life more difficult as coal permits were cancelled, electricity supplies slashed, Dublin trams paralysed and train services reduced to one or two a week. De Valera had refused to let himself be pushed around and if in the rest of the world admiration was grudgingly accorded, it was unbounded in Ireland. His electoral position was even further strengthened by the split in the Labour party and the trade union movement over the controversial figure of James ('Big Jim') Larkin and the 'Red scare' campaign run by his powerful trade-union rival, William O'Brien, with the willing help of the Catholic *Standard*.

It was sweet music in Irish ears to hear the redoubtable George Bernard Shaw publicly admitting he was wrong about de Valera and neutrality. Shaw told the *Daily Sketch* that the suggestion of economic sanctions against Eire was 'outrageous' and 'inexcusable'. He continued: 'I tried hard before the United States entered the war to get de Valera to abandon neutrality and join in. I told him he would not get away with it. He didn't think he would either but he described my suggestion as contemptible . . . but de Valera did get away with it.' A little later in the Scottish weekly, *Forward*, Shaw generously repeated his admission that he had underestimated de Valera's ability to get away with the 'crack-brained line' of neutrality and concluded admiringly: 'Howbeit, that powerless little cabbage garden called Ireland wins in the teeth of all the mighty Powers. Erin go Bragh!'

Notes to this chapter are on pp 182–3

Chapter 10

'We Had Him on a Plate'

Hitler's death was announced in the Irish newspapers on 2 May 1945 and later that day de Valera, accompanied by Walshe of External Affairs, called on Hempel at the German legation in Northumberland Road 'to express condolence'. By this stage the full horror of Belsen, Buchenwald and other Nazi extermination camps was being revealed to the outside world by the advancing allied armies and de Valera's call aroused an outcry in Britain, the USA, Canada and other countries. It was in vain that Irish officials pointed out that de Valera had made a similar call following the death of President Roosevelt some weeks before and had paid public tribute to him in the Dail, so as the head of a neutral government it was only correct diplomatic procedure for him to call on Hempel.

In fact both Walshe and Boland in External Affairs had practically begged de Valera not to make the call as they foresaw only too clearly what the international reaction would be, but he was not to be dissuaded. In a personal letter to Brennan in Washington, de Valera defended his action:

> I have noted that my call on the German Minister on the announcement of Hitler's death was played up to the utmost. I expected this. I could have had a diplomatic illness but, as you know, I would scorn that sort of thing ... So long as we retained our diplomatic relations with Germany, to have failed to call upon the German representative would have been an act of unpardonable discourtesy to the German nation and to Dr Hempel himself. During the whole of the war, Dr Hempel's conduct was irreproach-

able. He was always friendly and invariably correct – in marked contrast with Gray. I certainly was not going to add to his humiliation in the hour of defeat.[1]

He went on to say that such formal acts of courtesy were never meant to connote approval or disapproval of the policies of the state in question. So well might de Valera defend his action on the grounds of logic and diplomatic protocol. On any other grounds it was an appalling blunder, and there can be few Irish people today who do not feel a sense of shame that sympathy was expressed in their name on the death of Hitler. According to diplomatic usage, de Valera was not even obliged to have called on Hempel as the death had not at that stage been officially confirmed and all Hempel and his staff knew was what they had heard on a radio. One can appreciate de Valera's wish to make a gesture to Hempel in the bitterness of defeat, but such a gesture could and should have been made in a private, personal manner and not by publicly associating the Irish people with an expression of sympathy for the death of a tyrant responsible for the murder of millions. The fact that neutral Portugal ordered two days of mourning attracted less attention.

A week later Germany surrendered and through the Irish government Hempel handed over the legation building to the allied representatives in Dublin. A group of students at Trinity College celebrated the allied victory by flying the British, American, Russian, French and Irish flags on the roof of the university. The crowd gathered outside in busy College Green took grave exception to the fact that the Irish flag was at the bottom of the mast, and they were only prevented from storming the college by police baton charges. Some of the mob then went on a minor rampage in the city smashing windows in Maffey's office, the American legation, the Wicklow Hotel and Jammet's restaurant, these last two being regarded as Ascendancy and therefore pro-British haunts. The Irish government apologised to Maffey and Gray, and the Trinity College authorities apologised to the government for the unpleasant incident. In fact the Trinity students, most of whom were Protestant, had their own unit of the Local Defence Force in the college during the war years and it was unfortunate that the over-exuberant action of a handful should have given a misleading impression.

The newspaper censorship was immediately lifted and, freed from the restraints of almost six years of battling with Mr Aiken and his officials, the *Irish Times* burst forth with an indictment of the way the Press censorship system had been handled declaring: 'We have been living and speaking in conditions of unspeakable humiliation.' The paper revealed that it had been singled out by Mr Aiken for especially severe treatment, and was the only one that was obliged to submit to the censor in advance every inch of printed matter including the small advertisements. The censorship had certainly overstepped its powers when it had demanded that in a routine announcement of services for the Kingstown Presbyterian Church, the word Kingstown should be replaced by Dun Laoghaire which had been the official name for the town for more than twenty years. The fact that the church was entitled to keep its original title regardless of the change in the town's name was not conceded by the censor. The quarrel went deeper than this particular incident as in those days the *Irish Times* was closely identified with the shrinking numbers of Protestant landed gentry and ex-servicemen with pro-Unionist sympathies who found de Valera's ideal of a Gaelic and Catholic Ireland rather repugnant. Nevertheless, under the editorship of R. M. Smyllie, the *Irish Times* fully supported the neutrality policy although cynics would say that under the censorship system it had little choice. To get around the more absurd restrictions laid down by the censor (such as the suppression of any news item or even death notice which revealed the presence of Irishmen in the British forces), the paper resorted to ingenious devices which made Dublin smile but infuriated the censorship when it found out how it had been tricked. Thus, to inform its readers of the survival of a former member of the paper's staff who had joined the Royal Navy and whose ship was sunk, the paper solemnly reported that Mr 'X' was safe and sound after a 'boating accident in the Mediterranean'. The censor's interference with the death notices of Irishmen killed in action while serving with the British forces was rather spiteful. No reference to military rank or the manner of death was permitted and in one case even the second part of the Biblical quotation: 'Greater love than this no man hath than that he lay down his life for his friends', was struck out. In the Dail, Aiken defended this action by ponderously declaring: 'We have also to prevent some people not interested in men who die making use of obituary notices to forward propaganda in favour of the belligerent they desire to favour'.[2]

On 13 May Churchill gave his victory speech, but in his moment of triumph Irish neutrality still rankled and he gave vent to his bitterness:

> The sense of envelopment, which might at any moment turn to strangulation, lay heavy upon us . . . This was indeed a deadly moment in our life and if it had not been for the loyalty and friendship of Northern Ireland we should have been forced to come to close quarters with Mr de Valera or perish for ever from the earth. However, with a restraint and poise to which, I say, history will find few parallels, His Majesty's Government never laid a violent hand upon them though at times it would have been quite easy and quite natural, and we left the Dublin Government to frolic with the Germans and later with the Japanese representatives to their hearts' content.

The humiliation of this widely publicised Churchillian rebuke following on the controversial call by de Valera on Hempel caused anger and resentment in Ireland. There was pride in the revelation that the contingent of southern Irishmen serving in the British forces had won a total of 780 decorations, including eight Victoria Crosses (twice as many as for Northern Ireland and nearly as many as Canada with three times the population). But amid the general rejoicing at the end of the war was a fear that Ireland was now going to be ostracised by the victors for her official neutrality, a fear which was increased by the exclusion of the neutrals from the inauguration of the United Nations Organisation at San Francisco, the adverse publicity for de Valera's gesture on Hitler's death and now Churchill's contemptuous sneer. Gray had visualised Ireland finding herself in just such a situation two years earlier and that was why he had worked so hard to get de Valera explicitly on the record as refusing an appeal from the allies to help their war effort by removing the Axis missions from Dublin.

For four days the country waited impatiently for de Valera to give Churchill his answer and at last on the night of 17 May he made a radio broadcast to the nation.[3] The studied delay before replying and the moderate, statesmanlike tone he then adopted gave de Valera a psychological and moral advantage of which he took full use. He began by saying that he knew the kind of answer he was expected to make and the kind of answer that first sprang to the lips of every man of Irish blood who heard or read the Churchill speech. He knew the reply he himself would have given a quarter of a century ago, but he had deliberately decided that that was not the reply he was going to make that night. De Valera then pressed home unerringly his attack on the flank where Churchill had left himself open:

> Mr Churchill makes it clear that, in certain circumstances, he would have violated our neutrality and that he would justify his action by Britain's necessity. It seems strange to me that Mr Churchill does not see that this, if accepted, would mean that Britain's necessity would become a moral code and that when this necessity became sufficiently great, other people's rights were not to count.

De Valera then went on to give Churchill full credit for successfully resisting the temptation to attack Ireland and that instead of adding another horrid chapter to the already bloodstained record of Anglo-Irish relations, he had 'advanced the cause of international morality an important step'. It was a masterly touch on de Valera's part – first to expose the untenable moral basis on which Churchill had attacked Irish neutrality and then magnanimously to congratulate him for not committing a Hitler-like aggression on a virtually defenceless country. De Valera then took the opportunity to pay tribute to Neville Chamberlain whose decision to give back the Treaty Ports had made Irish neutrality possible and forecast that he would yet 'find the honoured place in British history which is due to him, as certainly he will find it in any fair record of the relations between Britain and ourselves'.

To make his case for Irish neutrality as persuasive as possible to British ears, de Valera went on to draw an analogy between the partition of Ireland and what would have happened if Germany had defeated and occupied Britain but then after many years withdrew, while continuing to occupy the six strategic southern counties commanding the Dover Straits. Supposing then, de Valera continued, that Germany found herself engaged in a war in which she could show she was on the side of the freedom of a number of small nations, would Mr Churchill 'lead this partitioned England to join with Germany in a crusade? I do not think Mr Churchill would'.

As an analogy it was not convincing – even to many Irish ears. Britain's 'occupation' of the six north-eastern counties of Ireland was not quite so arbitrary and was to some extent based on the obvious fact that a total withdrawal from Ireland in 1921 would have precipitated a civil war between north and south which neither Dublin nor London could have quelled without fearful killing and which would have made the civil war that did break out in the south look like a skirmish.

But this analogy allowed de Valera to reach the emotional climax of his reply to Churchill and ensure its instant and rapturous acceptance throughout the country. He went on:

> Mr Churchill is proud of Britain's stand alone, after France had fallen and before America entered the war.
>
> Could he not find in his heart the generosity to acknowledge that there is a small nation that stood alone, not for one year or two, but for several hundred years against aggression; that endured spoliations, famines, massacres in endless succession; that was clubbed many times into insensibility, but that each time on returning [to] consciousness, took up the fight anew; a small nation that could never be got to accept defeat and has never surrendered her soul?

When de Valera left the Radio Eireann studio in the General Post Office building in O'Connell Street after finishing the broadcast, crowds had already gathered in the street to cheer and acclaim him. His secretary, Kathleen O'Connell, recorded that the telephone kept ringing all night and telegrams and letters poured in for days afterwards. When de Valera entered the Dail the next day there was, according to his biographers, Longford and O'Neill, an unprecedented demonstration of enthusiasm and they add the comment: 'Never had he spoken so clearly for the nation and never had the nation been so proud of him.'

For the Dominions Office in London which had been enjoying de Valera's discomfiture on the world scene following the gaffe of the call on Hempel, Churchill's attack on Irish neutrality and the opening it gave to de Valera to regain lost prestige was the last thing they wanted. Cranborne, the Dominions Secretary, had already several months before in a memorandum for the war cabinet advised against Eire being allowed to join the United Nations because her lack of co-operation had 'put her quite out of court'.[4] He went on to warn that such exclusion might be resented by the other Dominions and he cited Canada's criticism of the American and British notes the previous year calling for the removal of the Axis missions. Now Churchill's outburst risked having a similar effect.

Maffey had been asked for an assessment of the exchange of broadcasts and he admitted that he found it a difficult task.[5] He himself had been pursuing towards Eire the policy approved by the Dominions

Office which was usually described as the 'absent treatment'. This policy, he continued, had yielded good results but the prime minister 'handling world problems on a vast stage, finds it expedient from time to time to come into collision with that policy, thereby producing local reactions here which may seem regrettable to those on the spot but which no doubt serve a useful purpose in another and higher dimension. If milk happens to be spilt here it would be presumptuous on my part to suggest any criticism of the hand which spilt it.'

Maffey then went back on the events of recent weeks to illustrate in diplomatic fashion just how ill-advised the Churchill intervention had been. After de Valera's call on Hempel, Maffey wrote, the public mind was too stunned to react quickly, but overnight there came the collapse of the Reich and with the sudden end of censorship there came atrocity stories and pictures of the concentration camps. In the public mind, 'Mr de Valera's condolences gradually took on a smear of turpitude, and for the first time, and at a critical time, a sense of disgust slowly manifested itself and a growing feeling that Mr de Valera had blundered into a clash with the ideals of decency and right and was leading away from realities.'

For Maffey further proof of the extent de Valera had wrong-footed himself was provided by the Canadian High Commissioner, John Kearney, 'a Catholic of Irish origin who, as is well known, inclines to take the kindly view of Irish shortcomings'. Kearney had called on Maffey on 17 May, the morning after de Valera's reply to Churchill, and he told Maffey he was sending a cable to Canada on the following lines:

> On Saturday, May 12th, I called on Mr. Walshe at the Department of External Affairs to show him a few cuttings from Canadian papers about de Valera's blunder. I told him that for me personally, who had always striven to be helpful, de Valera's action was a slap in the face. The consequences of these condolences for Hitler could not fail to be serious in Canada. I found the atmosphere of the Department profoundly depressed. Walshe even vaguely mooted some idea of apology. It was evident that the tide of public opinion was rising.
>
> Mr. Kearney then went on to say to me 'We had him on a plate. We had him where we wanted him. But look at the papers this morning!'

People in southern Ireland who lived near the border were able to watch the bonfires blazing a few miles away on northern hillsides where

Victory in Europe Day was being joyfully celebrated. But if the Irish north of the border could celebrate a victory in which they had played an active part, what were the Irish south of the border to celebrate? An allied victory over Germany? The victory of democracy over totalitarianism? The neutral who deliberately stands aside from the struggle can hardly hail the victory of one side or bemoan the defeat of the other. He can of course rejoice in the restoration of peace, and this was the overwhelming sentiment of the Irish people in May 1945. But there must have been many who, seeing at last the evil of the fascist ideologies and the terrible price which the democracies had to pay to crush it, asked themselves 'should we not have been fighting alongside the other democracies in this struggle, the outcome of which meant freedom or slavery?'

It was a question which had been flung at neutral Ireland many times throughout the war – and not just by those such as Churchill who were deeply prejudiced through longstanding opposition to the very idea of Irish independence. In July 1943, Herbert Morrison, the Labour Home Secretary, said in a speech that Irish neutrality not only indicated a state of mind between Britain and Eire which was long known and understood, but, he went on: 'The tragic thing is that Eire, a country which has fought many a battle for what it conceived to be the cause of liberty in one way or another, should have stood aside neutral, indifferent to one of the most dramatic and fateful struggles in the history of all mankind. That does not stand up too well in the history of the nations.'

The American historian, Professor Commager, had been lecturing in Cambridge during the war and had been invited to Dublin by the Irish Institute for International Affairs, a group of pro-allied academics and politicians who incurred one of de Valera's rare outbursts of temper in the Dail. He had found himself in the embarrassing position of having to defend the government's ban on such distinguished speakers invited by the institute as Jan Masaryk and Señor de Madariaga. Professor Commager had taken advantage of his visit to Dublin to write a long indictment of Irish neutrality in the *New York Times* arguing that the Irish people had 'missed out somehow on the greatest moral issue of modern history'.

In an article in the *Sunday Times* in February 1944, Lord Crewe analysed the stance of the neutrals, but while he found that the neutrality of Switzerland, Sweden, Portugal, Spain and Turkey was justified,

'Ireland's unique refusal to stand by the Commonwealth and Empire has shocked public opinion because the issue was not one of disputed rights or wounded pride but of simple right and wrong.'

The fate of Poland, the *casus belli*, and other eastern European countries in the post-war settlement made a mockery of the attempt to indict the neutrals on moral grounds for not joining in the war on the side of the alliance which included the totalitarian state which had ruthlessly absorbed the Baltic states, half of Poland and had started the war as a tacit ally of Hitler. Fervent Catholic though he was, de Valera had never any time for the 'Christian crusade' argument in favour of abandoning neutrality, and the entry of the USSR into the war showed the absurdity of such an argument. Lord Crewe's simplistic 'right and wrong' approach to Irish neutrality was based, of course, on the presumed obligations of Dominion status, overlooking the fact that not only had Ireland been forced under threat of 'immediate and terrible war' to accept Dominion status in 1921 instead of the full independence which she wanted, but that Britain had, since the Statute of Westminster, conceded that Dominion status included the freedom to decide not to declare war.

The charge that Irish neutrality was both moral and physical cowardice naturally rankled with the men who were proud to have defied the British Empire and to have won. De Valera tried to convince critics such as James Dillon that neutrality, 'if you are sincere about it, means that you will have to fight for your life against one side or the other – whichever attacks you . . . Neutrality is not a cowardly policy if you really mean to defend yourself if attacked. Other nations have not gone crusading until they were attacked.' On the same occasion in the Dail, de Valera seized gratefully on a letter by Captain Henry Harrison in answer to Professor Commager's attack on Irish neutrality. As de Valera pointed out, Harrison, a one-time supporter of Parnell and Home Rule had been fighting in a British uniform in France in 1916 and winning the Military Cross while de Valera and his fellow 'rebels' had been fighting the British army in Dublin in Easter Week. In Irish politics he and Harrison were poles apart but on neutrality, the former British officer and the 1916 insurgent were in total agreement. Harrison demolished Commager's argument so effectively that de Valera could not refrain from reading it into the Dail record. The kernel of it went as follows:

You proclaim that the Irish people have 'missed out somehow on the greatest moral issue of modern history' . . . Presumably when Britain and France declared war upon the Axis in September, 1939, 'the greatest moral issue in modern history' came into being but Russia continued to 'miss out' on it until Hitler invaded her territory in June, 1941, and America herself 'missed out on the greatest moral issue of modern history' for two and a quarter years until December 1941, when Japan struck her the assassin blow at Pearl Harbor. These two great leviathan Powers were no voluntary crusaders leaping into the arena in unreflecting and disinterested enthusiasm for high moral principle. They had made no move when others were wantonly attacked. They remained neutral when Denmark and Norway, Holland and Belgium, Jugoslavia and Greece were, in turn, ravaged and enslaved. They fought because they had to, because they had no choice left, because they were attacked, because being attacked, they needs must fight or submit to a conqueror's yoke. And little Ireland was not attacked. That is the difference. That is the sole difference. For there is nothing more certain than that Ireland also would have fought back if she had been attacked.[6]

There was no gainsaying this argument which Harrison expressed so forcefully. No country jumped into World War II out of high moral motives. When Britain and France declared war on Germany in support of Poland, between them in naval, land and air forces they outnumbered those of the Third Reich but did virtually nothing to aid Poland in those crucial weeks in September while the Poles fought gallantly on both fronts and waited in vain for the promised help. In the closing stages of the war, with the allied armies encircling Germany, there would have been little or no risk in jumping on the bandwaggon and becoming a belligerent on the victorious side as many South American countries did under diplomatic and economic pressure from the United States, but de Valera scorned such behaviour and few will say he was wrong although it cost Ireland eleven years' exclusion from the United Nations because of the Soviet veto. The Soviet delegate argued rather illogically that because Ireland had been neutral, she was not a 'peace-loving nation'.

But if there can be little argument about the correctness of Ireland's decision to remain neutral given all the circumstances, one can regret the resultant side-effect which was a feeling of smugness and moral superiority which could take quite objectionable forms. This moral blurring which took place was inevitable given the severity of the censorship, and de Valera's constant public expressions of gratitude to

L

—*by Illingworth.*

Grave offence was taken in Dublin to this Daily Mail *cartoon by Illingworth showing de Valera riding stubbornly on a donkey to disaster while the former neutrals, Norway, Belgium, Holland, Denmark and Rumania, warn him from behind the barbed wire of a Nazi concentration camp of his folly. This cartoon was part of the strident British and American Press campaign attacking Irish neutrality which followed Churchill's speech in the House of Commons on 5 November 1940 complaining at not having the use of the Irish ports.*

the Almighty for his favoured treatment of the Irish people. Maffey, not unnaturally, was irritated by this 'holier than thou' attitude which he encountered and in a despatch in October 1942, looking ahead to the general election due the following year, he referred to 'the difficulties of any government here which might endeavour to swing over a public which has been drugged by the censorship, appalled by stories and some small experience of "blitz" and which, when it thinks at all, considers that it is under God's special protection and is called upon to suffer only negligible hardships owing to a war in which wicked and violent men have been plunged as a punishment of sin'.

The American note affair, presented as a diplomatic triumph for de Valera, helped to increase the air of unreality which neutrality plus censorship was spreading, and even the normally acquiescent parliamentary opposition expressed its unease through the Fine Gael front-bench member, Dr O'Higgins, when he complained: 'We are bringing up a generation blissfully unconscious of facts, in imbecile ignorance, thinking that in a world war a declaration, plus a comparatively insignificant army is sufficient to keep a country free from war ... We have magnified our immunity from war and our neutral position into a major Government achievement and not only that, but an achievement due to one great man.'[7]

The 'great man' himself can have had no illusions about the fate of Ireland if the Nazi new order triumphed, but his rigorous view of neutrality would never permit him to give the Irish people the benefit of his superior knowledge and as a result his speeches invariably presented the opposing belligerents as moral equals or perhaps amoral equals. Many Irish people who fully approved of neutrality as the only possible policy for Ireland, found this moral equation of the belligerents distasteful and at times infuriating. De Valera believed he was being logical in observing mental as well as political neutrality. He told the Dail:

> What we have to do, as a people, is to rely on our right, to rely upon the goodness of our cause, to hope that the Almighty will be favourable to us as He has been up to the present, and to do everything we can to deserve it, and, whatever the future brings, to accept it and to do our best to minimise any dangers that may be in it. But we are not going into the position that Deputy Dillon wants to put us into. He would have the whole Irish nation put into this position – he wants us to go on wishing that one side will win, to go on wishing and shouting about it.

On occasions de Valera also made it clear that for those who felt that strongly about the moral obligation for Ireland to help the allied cause, there was a simple remedy – to join the British forces. Once he snapped at Dillon that if he had felt the way Dillon talked he would have gone off and fought himself.

On the question of supplies of vital imports such as oil, petrol, coal and wheat, Ireland could not have survived without British and American goodwill. De Valera's references in 1941 to a 'double blockade', whereby both belligerents in blockading each other were also blockading Ireland, was another unjustified equation which stung the British and the Americans all the more deeply inasmuch as they believed that by being deprived of the Irish Atlantic ports the difficulties of supplying Ireland as well as Britain with food and vital materials were thereby greatly increased. Of the twenty Irish ships lost because of belligerent action and the seventeen foreign ships on charter, there will never be absolutely foolproof evidence on the responsibility but there are reasonable grounds to assume that most of these shipping losses were due to German action. In the one case where there was proof of British responsibility, the strafing of the *Kerlogue*, the British government admitted RAF involvement and an offer of compensation was made, but on the Irish side it had to be admitted that the vessel was well off the course which was laid down for neutral shipping plying between the British Isles and Portugal. The economic pressure which was applied by Britain as described in Chapter 5 was certainly not a blockade, but for de Valera's view of neutrality it was more fitting to be blockaded by both sides as then the Irish people need not be disturbed by doubts on the morality of the struggle they were witnessing from the sidelines.

It would be unjust to de Valera not to acknowledge that his maintenance of Irish neutrality throughout an extremely difficult period was a considerable diplomatic and political triumph. At the time it certainly seemed the correct decision to take and while one can criticise details of how neutrality was enforced, it succeeded and that is the ultimate test of any policy. At one stage in June 1940 when the German armies seemed invincible and it was only a matter of time before they overran Britain, and with Ireland's fate equally uncertain, de Valera in a broadcast warned that if the violation of Irish territory promised an advantage to either side, then 'our territory will be violated, our country will be made a cockpit, our homes will be levelled and our people slaughtered'. It was perhaps the most sombre and alarming prospect which he held up before the people during the whole period and he went on to emphasise that the 'greatest peril' in that extremely dangerous time was partition.

But he was wrong. It was because of partition that when later in the year the British merchant shipping losses rose to an intolerable level, the Royal Navy and Royal Air Force were able to begin mounting a counter-assault on the U-boat wolf pack in the North Atlantic from bases in Northern Ireland. If these bases had not been available, and the shipping losses had continued to mount, there can be no doubt that the British pressure for the southern ports would have mounted also and the point would have been reached where Churchill would have seen the alternatives as seizure of the ports or starvation. There was little doubt as to which course he would have adopted.

The other side of the partition coin was Churchill's attempt to bring de Valera into the war with eventual reunification as the bait. We have seen that Churchill had misgivings about the plan if it meant coercing the northern Unionists, but the situation was fairly desperate and not long before he had offered France an Anglo-French union in a bid to rally the disintegrating government of Reynaud and the French Empire to a continuance of the struggle.

It was a cruel choice with which to confront de Valera: a united Ireland but at the price of war with, at that time, an all-conquering Germany. Churchill prophesied that if Eire continued to remain neutral throughout the war – and he thought it unlikely – then 'a gulf will have opened between Northern and Southern Ireland which will be impossible to bridge in this generation'. This forecast has been only too true. With the advantage of hindsight, was de Valera wrong not to throw in his lot with Britain in her 'finest hour' and join with the separated northern brethren in the struggle to free Europe from the tyranny of the dictators? Walshe in External Affairs saw in those dark days of 1940 that if Eire played her cards right a more promising way to Irish unity lay in an accommodation with a victorious Germany. Fortunately, de Valera did not dally with that temptation, strong though it may have been. Neutrality more accurately reflected the mood and deepest feelings of the Irish people in the south than an artificial unity uneasily forged in the crucible of a world war. De Valera, and indeed other politicians, sensed the strength of that feeling in a people still groping for their new identity a mere twenty years after the shock of independence and the tragic civil war which was its aftermath. Even de Valera with his vast prestige could scarcely have wrought the change in that dumb but powerful urge among the people for peace at any price which would have been necessary to lead the country into a war they did not understand. For Ireland, out on the western rim of an embattled Europe, neutrality seemed the only way to ensure survival and to everyone's amazement it worked.

It worked, not because of de Valera, important though his role was as leader of the country at that critical time, but because the invasion of Ireland never became a vital interest for either belligerent. The huge stocks of German military maps of Ireland found by the allies in Brussels in 1944 and the manuals on how to treat the natives (their 'lack of hygiene' was noted) were paralleled by the lorry loads of maps which the British army in Northern Ireland had ready for the day it might be called on to cross the border either to help the Irish resist a German invasion or to take the ports by force if they had become in Maffey's phrase, 'a matter of life or death'.

With hindsight it can be seen that the likelihood of invasion was stronger from the allied side than the German since the latter, as we saw in Chapter 4, even at the height of their successes, did not have the naval superiority to launch such an operation. The British war cabinet, on the other hand, had seriously to consider the possibility of an invasion of neutral Eire on various occasions, but up to the end of 1941 the thought of the resultant unfavourable reaction from the USA and the Commonwealth was an effective deterrent. By the time American opinion was a less inhibiting factor, the southern Irish ports had not the same importance for the anti-submarine warfare and the secret military liaison between the British and Irish staffs had replaced in large part the earlier mutual distrust.

But within this larger geo-political framework, de Valera's role was of the greatest importance. His decision that the neutrality policy would be 'benevolent' towards the allies but rigorously legal towards the Germans, was finely calculated to allow for the basically pro-allied feeling in Ireland which he shared and also for the inescapable geographical reality of being part of the British Isles.

Senior army officers who had been opposed to de Valera and the republican side during the civil war twenty years previously have paid tribute to the firmness with which he conducted the neutrality policy and confessed to the author that they never thought they would one day have cause to admire to such an extent their one-time adversary. Doubtless the 'free state' elements in the senior ranks were impressed by de Valera's fairly ruthless treatment of the IRA (six executions, three hunger-strike deaths, over five hundred interned, including eighteen women, and about six hundred convicted under the Offences Against the State Act). The discreet bending of neutrality in favour of the allies would also have met with the approval of the officer corps, most of whom hoped for an allied victory.

Because of the non-availability of Irish government papers, it is difficult to assess how de Valera conducted the neutrality policy on a day-to-day basis. It is doubtful, however, if he confided many of the details to his ministers, some of whose wives were notoriously indiscreet and whose telephones had to be tapped. He had the great advantage of being his own foreign minister and the result was that the neutrality policy was largely decided and conducted by de Valera himself with the close collaboration of Joe Walshe and F. H. Boland in the Department of External Affairs. Frank Aiken was a close confidant of de Valera and we have seen how he was entrusted with the mission to the United States, but as even his friends believed him to be pro-German in his sympathies, it is unlikely that de Valera could have risked taking Aiken always fully into his confidence.

The military liaison arrangements between General Franklyn in the north and General McKenna in the south needed extremely careful handling as Hempel was no fool and must have had some idea of what was going on. De Valera kept a close eye on this collaboration between the military staffs, and McKenna reported to him personally after each meeting. He found that de Valera was more interested in indications of changes of mood or intention among the British towards the south than in the actual details of their co-operation. The appointment of Major Vivion de Valera as a liaison officer to General Franklyn also enabled his father to be fully informed, and as far as possible the more politically sensitive aspects of this bizarre north–south relationship were known only to a small caucus of the more senior staff officers as well as to de Valera himself.

The most nerve-wracking time during those difficult years must have been the second half of 1940. France had fallen, the German armies seemed invincible and the conquest of Britain only a matter of time. De Valera was almost blind and we have seen the enormous pressures which were exerted on him as reports of impending invasion, now by the Germans, now by the British, flowed in. One day Malcolm MacDonald was in Dublin urging him to barter neutrality for shadowy unity. The next day Hempel was in his office with barely veiled threats that publicity for the Held–Goertz case could not be tolerated and holding out the bait of a victorious Germany's help for the reunification of Ireland. It was at this time that Hempel reported to Berlin on de Valera's 'shattered confidence' and Walshe was starting to anticipate a certain British defeat, but de Valera's nerve did not fail and Hempel was never able to report anything other than his unwavering adherence to neutrality. By November of the same year Churchill was again complaining bitterly about not having the use of the ports, the British Press was hinting at a forcible takeover and Ribbentrop was offering the *cadeau empoisonné* of captured British arms and equipment. This time de Valera riposted publicly to Churchill with his stirring Dail speech on readiness to defend neutrality to the death, and he cleverly played for time before refusing the German offer. Yet the year was not to end without successive British and German invasion scares while de Valera was undergoing surgery to restore his sight. This was *his* 'finest hour' but few could know it.

The American note affair retains some puzzling aspects in spite of the publication of the various exchanges. Regardless of repeated assurances from Gray that an ultimatum was not intended, de Valera chose to react as if failure to accede to the demand to expel the Axis diplomats was going to precipitate an Allied invasion. It is interesting that de Valera was remarkably restrained during the interview with Gray when the latter presented the note, while he was much more agitated during the subsequent interviews with Maffey and Kearney. It is hard not to believe that this agitation was feigned and was a deliberate part of the war of nerves which he embarked upon and which included the full-scale alert of the entire defence forces. If this were the case, de Valera's ploy certainly worked as Gray and Maffey, as we have seen, were immediately put on the defensive. It is also possible, however, that de Valera genuinely feared an invasion of American troops from Northern Ireland and wished to demonstrate that whatever Gray might have advised Washington, the Irish resistance would not be a token one but a stubborn resistance for as long as the outnumbered, outgunned Irish army could hold out. American intentions were always deeply suspect to de Valera and his ministers. Although there was little love lost on the British, the Irish felt they knew where they stood with them while the Americans were distrusted and believed to be 'dangerous'.

The final episode of the call on Hempel to express sympathy on the death of Hitler was probably the most controversial of de Valera's actions throughout the whole period. Although in the author's view it was and is deeply regrettable that the Irish people should have been associated with such a gesture, it can also be viewed as a rather perverted example of de Valera's consistency and one which required not a little courage to carry through knowing the outraged reaction which would follow. De Valera also showed a more admirable courage in refusing allied demands for the immediate handing over of Hempel and his staff and the small group of German spies who had been interned. Instead he offered the diplomats asylum and Hempel and his wife were helped by the government to try and set up a confectionery business. An agreement was reached with the allies that the spies would not be handed over until two years had elapsed and passions had cooled. It was tragic that when the two years were up, Goertz should have committed suicide rather than return to Germany although he had been given solemn assurances that his life was not in danger.

By then power was slipping from de Valera and his tired government as they tried to combat the unpopularity caused by the post-war shortages and the worsening economic situation. A little over six months later Fianna Fáil's sixteen-year spell in government came to an end. It was the succeeding coalition government of Fine Gael, Labour and the new radical, republican party, Clann na Poblachta which refused the American invitation to join the Atlantic Alliance in January 1949 and which formally declared the state to be a republic later that year, thus removing once and for all the ambiguity about whether the country was in or out of the Commonwealth. De Valera had cleverly exploited this ambiguity during the war and the attitude of the Dominions during the American note incident showed how valuable it could be. But perhaps it was only a de Valera with his awesome ability, when the occasion arose, to strain the meaning of certain key words beyond the comprehension of most other mortals, who could have continued to have derived profit from such a situation.

The refusal of the coalition government to join the Atlantic Alliance was a logical extension of wartime neutrality as in both cases partition was put forward as an insuperable obstacle to the abandonment of neutrality. Later Fianna Fáil governments under Mr Lemass and Mr Lynch did not see themselves bound, however, by what has virtually become a neutrality myth. There were hints during the Lemass period that membership of NATO just might be considered, and it was during this time that the firm decision to apply for full membership of the European Economic Community was taken although such a decision more or less implied that at some future date Ireland would have to take a defence commitment as the community moved towards closer political union. When accused by opponents of EEC membership that they were destroying the country's neutrality tradition, the Fianna Fáil leaders replied that the wartime neutrality was merely *ad hoc* and

M

not ideological like that of Switzerland and Sweden. And they were right. Neutrality had never been a dogma for de Valera who had not opposed that part of the disputed 1921 treaty which handed over the ports and naval defence to Britain, and later he fully supported the collective security aim of the League of Nations and sanctions against aggressors such as Italy. De Valera's decision to keep Ireland neutral was an *ad hoc* one, but he carried it through so successfully and brilliantly that for many people, including his political opponents, neutrality became a veritable creed. And whatever their governments, it is a creed to which the Irish people have become closely attached and will not lightly lay aside.

Notes to this chapter are on p 183

Notes

———————

The British war cabinet minutes and related documents for the period of World War II were released for public inspection in 1972. The minutes are contained in the series CAB 65 and the related memoranda mainly in the series CAB 66. The Foreign Office political correspondence is filed in the series FO 371 and that for the Dominions Office under DO 35. For the German diplomatic papers the source has been *Documents on German Foreign Policy, 1918–45*, Series D, and for the American papers the series *Foreign Relations of the United States*. These will be referred to as DGFP and FRUS.

Chapter 1 (pp 11–23)

1 Cabinet minutes, 1 September 1939
2 Dail debates, Vol 74
3 Earl of Longford and Thomas O'Neill, *Eamon de Valera*, p 348
4 CAB 67, 1
5 Cabinet minutes, 31 October 1939, 8 November 1939
6 Paul Leverkuehn, *German Military Intelligence*, p 102
7 CAB 66, 1
8 'Lord Rugby Remembers', *Irish Times*, 3, 4 July 1962
9 CAB 66, 1
10 Ibid, WP (39) 34
11 DO 35, Box 1107
12 Lord Avon, *The Reckoning*, p 69
13 Nicholas Bethell, *The War Hitler Won*, p 242
14 FO 371, 23966
15 Ibid

Chapter 2 (pp 24–38)

1 Louis MacNeice, *Collected Poems 1925–48*

2 W. S. Churchill, *The Second World War*, Vol 1: *The Gathering Storm*, p 248
3 CAB 64, 34
4 Churchill, op cit, p 382
5 Cabinet minutes, 15 October 1939
6 Ibid, 18 October 1939
7 CAB 66, 2
8 *Survey of International Affairs 1935–36*
9 Dail debates, Vol 62
10 CAB 66, 2
11 CAB 67, 2
12 DGFP, Vol 8
13 Ibid

Chapter 3 (*pp 39–59*)

1 CAB 67, 6
2 Enno Stephan, *Spies in Ireland*, p 110
3 Quoted in Longford and O'Neill, p 365
4 CAB 66, 8
5 The author is indebted to Brigadier Clarke for allowing him to see the censored manuscript.
6 William Langer and S. Everett Gleason, *The World Crisis and American Foreign Policy*, Vol 1: *The Challenge to Isolation*, p 522
7 Longford and O'Neill, pp 370–1, give extracts from Cosgrave's interesting letter to de Valera offering the government his 'fullest support' for a change in the neutrality policy.
8 CAB 78, 33
9 CAB 66, 9 reproduces Chamberlain's memorandum for the war cabinet.
10 CAB 66, 10 reproduces Maffey's letter of 17 July, 1940.

Chapter 4 (*pp 60–77*)

1 *Irish Press*, 1 June 1940
2 DGFP, Vol 9. The other references in this chapter to German diplomatic documents are from Vols 9 to 13 inclusive.
3 Leverkuehn, op cit, p 103
4 Based on Hempel's report to Berlin
5 Langer and Gleason, op cit, p 522
6 Dr F. H. Boland later became one of Ireland's most distinguished diplomats and was a president of the United Nations General Assembly.
7 CAB 66, 10
8 Ronald Wheatley, *Operation Sea Lion*
9 *Irish Press*, 12 December 1940
10 Dail debates, Vol 81, 7 November 1940
11 Cabinet minutes, 21 November 1940
12 *Brassey's Naval Annual 1948*, 'Fuehrer's Conferences on Naval Affairs', 3 December 1940

Chapter 5 (pp 78–94)

1 Churchill, Vol 2: *Their Finest Hour*, p 614
2 Ibid
3 CAB 66, 14 reproduces the memorandum.
4 Cabinet minutes, 6 December 1940
5 CAB 67, 8 reproduces a series of memoranda giving the British view of the negotiations.
6 Cabinet minutes, 24 March 1941
7 CAB 66, 15
8 Dail debates, Vol 79, col 1767
9 Ibid, Vol 82, col 1588
10 DO 35, Box 1107
11 Dail debates, Vol 88, col 519ff
12 CAB 72, 25 has a voluminous file on how the economic pressure was applied to Ireland during the war years. Much of the material in this chapter is drawn from this file.
13 Basil Peterson, *Turn of the Tide*, gives an account of the setting up of Irish Shipping Ltd and its fortunes during the war.
14 DO 35, Box 1228
15 FO 371, 29108
16 *Irish Times*, 28 October 1972

Chapter 6 (pp 95–110)

1 FO 371, 29108
2 FRUS 1941, Vol 3
3 Longford and O'Neill, op cit, p 377 and Churchill, Vol 3: *The Grand Alliance*
4 John W. Blake in the official history, *Northern Ireland in the Second World War*, published in 1956 mentioned BTNI plans to move south in the event of a German invasion but made no reference at all to the liaison arrangement with the Irish defence forces. Probably as in the case of Dudley Clarke he was not allowed to.
5 DO 3 has a long list of files under the reference WX 30 dealing with 'Eire Defence' but many of them are marked 'Destroyed under Statute' or 'Closed until 1990'.
6 DO 35, Box 1109 (second part)
7 *Irish Press*, 8 April 1940
8 Langer and Gleason, op cit, p 484
9 *The Memoirs of Cordell Hull*, pp 1351ff
10 Longford and O'Neill, op cit, p 375
11 FO 371, 29108
12 Ibid
13 'Robert Brennan's Wartime Mission in Washington', *Irish Press*, April–May 1958

14 FO 371, 29108
15 DGFP, Vol 11
16 Cabinet minutes, 26 May 1941 and annexes
17 DO 35, Box 1228 gives the following breakdown of southern Irish who
    joined up in Belfast: Army 28,645; Royal Navy and Marines 483;
    Royal Air Force 9,426. It is claimed that the number of Irish who
    joined up in Britain cannot be accurately calculated as they would have
    given British addresses, but General Sir Hubert Gough in a letter to the
    London *Times* in August 1944 said that there were 165,000 next of kin
    Irish addresses.

Chapter 7 (pp 111–126)

1 Longford and O'Neill, op cit, pp 392–3
2 CAB 67, 9
3 FO 371, 32591. This file is the source for the exchanges between Churchill,
   Cranborne and Eden which follow.
4 Dail debates, Vol 84, col 1847ff
5 FRUS 1942, Vol 1
6 Hull, op cit
7 Interview
8 CAB 66, 34
9 An excellent account of the army during the emergency period is given in
   Irish Defence Forces Handbook 1968 edited by Commandant P. D.
   Kavanagh. For a similar account of the Marine Service, see Captain
   T. McKenna's detailed articles in *An Cosantoir*, April 1973.
10 DO 35, Box 1109 (Part One)
11 CAB 68, 8
12 An interesting, if romanticised, account of life at the Curragh for German
    internees is given in a book written by one of them who still lives in
    Ireland called in the French version, *Les Prisonniers de l'Île Verte*.
13 DO 35, Box 1108
14 CAB 66, 30
15 FO 371, 36002
16 Ibid

Chapter 8 (pp 127–138)

1 FRUS 1943, Vol 3, p 132
2 Hull, op cit
3 CAB 66, 40
4 CAB 66, 44
5 *Irish Press*, 28 April 1973
6 Dail debates, Vol 91, col 569

Chapter 9 (pp 139–159)

1 FRUS 1943, Vol 3, 13 December 1943

2 CAB 66, 46
3 Churchill, Vol 5, *Closing the Ring*
4 CAB 66, 48
5 FO 371, 42679
6 Ibid
7 FRUS 1944, Vol, 23 February 1944
8 FO 371, 42679
9 FRUS 1944, Vol 3, 1 March 1944
10 FO 371, 42679. This file provides most of the diplomatic material used in connection with the American note.
11 FO 371, 42680

Chapter 10 (pp 160–178)

1 Longford and O'Neill, op cit, p 411
2 Dail debates, Vol 96, col 2380
3 'Ireland's Stand', *De Valera Speeches*, p 89
4 CAB 66, 62
5 DO 35, Box 1229
6 Dail debates, Vol 91, col 2126
7 Ibid, Vol 94, col 1448

Bibliography

———

OFFICIAL PAPERS, RECORDS

Dail Debates, 1939–45, Dublin
Documents on German Foreign Policy, 1918–45, Series D
Foreign Relations of the United States, Diplomatic Papers, 1939–45
Seanad Debates, 1939–45, Dublin
War cabinet, Foreign Office and Dominions Office Papers

GENERAL

Bell, J. Bowyer. *The Secret Army* (1970)
Bethell, Nicholas. *The War Hitler Won* (1972)
Blake, J. W. *Northern Ireland in the Second World War* (Belfast, 1956)
Brassey's Naval Annual (1948)
The Diaries of Sir Alexander Cadogan, ed David Dilkes (1971)
Call to Arms, 'Authentic Historical Record of Ireland's Defence Forces' (Dublin, 1945)
Chatfield, Lord. *The Navy and Defence* (1942)
Churchill, W. S. *The Second World War,* Vols 1–6
Clarke, Dudley. *Seven Assignments* (1948)
Conor Cruise O'Brien Introduces Ireland, ed Owen Dudley Edwards, 'Ireland in International Affairs' (1969)
Coogan, T. P. *Ireland Since the Rising* (1966)
———. *The I.R.A.* (1970)
De Valera, Eamon. *Ireland's Stand* (Dublin)
Eden, Anthony. *Memoirs: The Reckoning* (1965)
Farago, Ladislas. *The Game of the Foxes* (New York, 1971)
Fell, W. R. *The Sea Our Shield* (1966)
Handbook of Local Security Forces (Dublin, 1940)
Harold Nicolson Diaries and Letters, ed Nigel Nicolson (1967)

Harrison, Henry. *The Neutrality of Ireland* (1942)

Hogan, V. P. *The Neutrality of Ireland in World War II* (Ann Arbor, 1953)

Hull, Cordell. *Memoirs* (1948)

Irish Army Handbook 1940 (Dublin)

Kavanagh, Commandant P. D. *Irish Defences Forces Handbook* (Dublin, 1968)

Langer, William and Gleason, S. Everett. *The World Crisis and American Foreign Policy* (1952)

Lawlor, Anthony T. *Irish Maritime Survey* (Dublin)

Leverkuehn, Paul. *German Military Intelligence* (1954)

Longford, Earl of and O'Neill, T. P. *Eamon de Valera* (Dublin, 1970)

Lyons, F. S. L. *Ireland Since the Famine* (1973)

McLachlan, Donald. *Room 39, A Study in Naval Intelligence*

Mansergh, Nicholas. *Survey of British Commonwealth Affairs, The Commonwealth and Neutrality Memoirs of Lord Ismay* (1960)

Nowlan, K. B. and Williams, T. Desmond, eds. *Ireland in the War Years and After, 1939–51* (Dublin, 1969)

O'Callaghan, S. *Jackboot in Ireland* (1958)

O'Connor Lysaght, D. R. *The Republic of Ireland* (Cork, 1970)

Peterson, Basil. *Turn of the Tide* (Dublin, 1962)

Stephan, Enno. *Spies in Ireland* (1965)

Toynbee, Arnold and Veronica, eds. *Survey of International Affairs 1939–46, The War and the Neutrals* (1956)

NEWSPAPERS, PERIODICALS

Boyd, Ernest. 'Ireland Between Two Stools', *Foreign Affairs* (January 1941)

Brennan, Robert. 'Wartime Mission in Washington', *Irish Press* (June-July 1958)

Dublin Opinion (1939–45)

Dwyer, Ryle. 'De Valera's Struggle for Irish Neutrality', *Irish Press* (26–30 November 1973)

Goertz, Hermann. 'Mission to Ireland', *Irish Times* (August 1947)

'Lord Rugby Remembers', *Irish Times* (3 July 1962)

McKenna, Captain T. 'Thank God We're Surrounded by Water', *An Cosantoir* (April 1973)

Murdoch, John. Interviews with Dr Hempel, *Sunday Press* (November-December 1963)

O'Brien, George. 'The Impact of the War on the Irish Economy', *Ireland Studies*, (March 1946)

Smyllie, R. M. 'Unneutral Neutral Eire', *Foreign Affairs* (January 1946)

Stuart, Francis. 'Frank Ryan in Germany', *The Bell* (November-December 1950)

Williams, T. Desmond. 'A Study in Neutrality', *The Leader* (January-April 1953)

——. 'Neutrality', *Irish Press* (June-July 1953)

Acknowledgements

———◆———

The author would like to thank particularly Dr F. H. Boland, Colonel Dan Bryan and Professor Desmond Williams who read most of my manuscript and offered valuable suggestions. Others who helped in various ways include: Frank Aiken, Sir John Betjeman, the late Gerry Boland, Colonel E. Butler, former Garda Commissioner Patrick Carroll, Brigadier Dudley Clarke, Helmut Clissman, Lt-General Sean Collins-Powell, Captain C. Costello, Major Vivion de Valera, James Dillon, Tom Earlie, Mrs Ffrench O'Carroll, George Fleischmann, Dr Hayes, Commandant P. Kavanagh, Charles Kelly, James Kitchen, Colonel Anthony Lawlor, Charles Lysaght, Colonel J. McCarthy, Frank MacDermot, Lt-General Daniel McKenna, General Peadar MacMahon, Commandant Sean Neligan, Sean Nunan, Sean O'Faolain, Thomas O'Neill, Commandant V. Savino, Maj-General T. P. Scott, Colonel P. Swan, the late Henning Thomsen, Count Tomacelli, Brigadier Max Tyler, William Warnock and Jack White.

Also gratefully acknowledged are the help and courtesy of the staffs of the Public Record Office and the British Museum Newspaper Section in London, the National Library and Trinity College Library in Dublin. The staffs of the libraries and art departments of the *Irish Press*, the *Irish Times* and *Irish Independent* were especially helpful – in particular, Tommy McCann, Terry Heery Liam Flynn and Tony Lennon.

Tim Pat Coogan, editor of the *Irish Press* was a constant source of encouragement, and the newspaper's London editor, Aidan Hennigan, was a generous host during frequent London visits. Thanks are also due to Wendy Pau who helped to prepare the manuscript.

Index